Touching the Reign of God

Touching the Reign of God

Bringing Theological Reflection to Daily Life

MARY SHARON MOORE

With a Foreword by
Francis Kelly Nemeck, O.M.I.

WIPF & STOCK · Eugene, Oregon

TOUCHING THE REIGN OF GOD
Bringing Theological Reflection to Daily Life

Wipf & Stock Publishers
199 West 8th Avenue, Suite 3
Eugene, Oregon 97401

www.wipfandstock.com

ISBN 13: 978-1-60608-197-6

Manufactured in the U.S.A.

When Jesus saw that [the scribe] answered wisely, he said to him, "You are not far from the kingdom of God." (Mark 12:34)

The kingdom of God is not coming with things that can be observed; nor will they say, "Look, here it is!" or "There it is!" For, in fact, the kingdom of God is within you. (Luke 17:21)

The word is near you, on your lips and in your heart. (Rom 10:8)

We declare to you what was from the beginning, what we have heard, what we have seen with our eyes, what we have looked at and touched with our hands . . . that you also may have fellowship with us; and truly our fellowship is with the Father and with his Son Jesus Christ. (1 John 1:1–3)

Contents

Foreword / ix

Introduction / xi

List of Abbreviations / xv

1 Throw Open the Door of Your Heart / 1

2 Your Redeeming Love / 7

3 Your Attitude Must Be Christ's / 19

4 Listen for the Lord / 25

5 No Longer for Ourselves / 31

6 Coming Up Short / 39

7 Let Me See Your Face / 44

8 Meditation on Three Words / 50

9 These Bones / 57

10 Triumph of Extreme Humility / 61

11 True Love / 67

12 Let My Prayer Arise / 72

13 Reconciled in Christ / 88

Index of Scripture / 93

Foreword

WORDS ARE particular. The title of this engaging theological reflection by Mary Sharon Moore is *Touching the Reign of God*. One might expect the title to read "*Kingdom* of God" rather than "*Reign* of God," for "kingdom" is by far the more popular translation of the Greek *basileia*, even though it is not necessarily the most accurate.

The choice of term, however, is deliberate and significant. Linguistically, "kingdom" is a noun that suggests a delineated territory. Yet, as these essays aptly illustrate, *basileia* in the context of Jesus' preaching functions more like a verb than a noun. The "reign of God" is fundamentally qualitative and relational rather than quantitative and cut and dried. The reign of God invites and challenges us to be drawn into a radically new way of being and of relating to self, to others, and indeed to all of creation. Each essay reminds us that the reign of God is alive and dynamic, a catalyst operating from within—like yeast. The reign of God illuminates—like a lamp on a stand. It is attentive—like prudent bridesmaids, and persistent—like a woman seeking a lost coin. The reign of God is compassionate—like the Samaritan traveler. The reign of God brims over with forgiveness—like the prodigal father of the impudent sons.

Jesus revealed the reign of God as already present, yet still coming. This collection of essays by Mary Sharon Moore reminds us that the reign of God is both within us and all around us.

As much as Jesus emphasized *basileia* in his preaching, he carefully avoided being called "king": He rode into Jerusalem on a donkey, not a chariot. He wore a crown of thorns rather than of gold. His scepter was a shepherd's staff, his throne a cross. It was not as king but as servant that Jesus celebrated his Passover.

The other key word in the title of this volume is "touching"—*Touching* the reign of God. Similar to "reign," the word "touch" is dynamic, alive. It connotes meeting, encounter, as we experience God's purging and transforming activity within us and all around us. Touching the reign of God means submitting to the gradual awakening within our consciousness of the imperative of divine love.

We touch God's reign because God's reign has first touched us and is already drawing us into an everlasting loving exchange.

Through these reflections we pray, Father, that your reign come, that your will be done on earth as in heaven. We pray, Father, that we be faithful witnesses and stewards of your reign, that we be trustworthy instruments of this transforming activity.

—Francis Kelly Nemeck, OMI
Lebh Shomea House of Prayer
Sarita, Texas
August 24, 2008

Introduction

I HAVE always been intrigued, haunted, and challenged by a passage in St. Mark's Gospel where, following a dispute between some Sadducees and Jesus, a scribe approaches Jesus and cuts to the heart of the matter. Teacher, he asks, "which commandment is the first of all?" By what law, he seems to ask, should I order my heart, my mind, my being, my doing? What truth is deserving enough and compelling enough for the right ordering of my life?

Jesus replies, "The first is, 'Hear O Israel: the Lord our God, the Lord is one; you shall love the Lord your God with all your heart, and with all your soul, and with all your mind, and with all your strength.'"

And for Jesus, that one great commandment could never be enough. As within the perfect communion of the Holy Trinity, so within the communion of human relationships. Jesus continues: "The second is this, 'You shall love your neighbor as yourself.'"

The scribe reflects on these words and speaks them back, disciple to Teacher. And we read, "When Jesus saw that he answered wisely, he said to him, 'You are not far from the kingdom of God'" (see Mark 12:28–34).

I am intrigued, haunted, challenged, because at the core of my being I know that Jesus' teaching is true.

I am haunted, because Jesus spells out so clearly the very simple, yet high-threshold way of life I must live when I say that I am his. And I know that I sorely miss the mark.

And I am challenged by the searingly accurate judgment, delivered with such compassion and encouragement: *You are not far from the kingdom of God.*

I don't want to be "not far" from the kingdom of God. I don't even want to be *near* the kingdom of God. I want to make my home in the kingdom of God and live every aspect of my life inside the reign of God.

The "kingdom" of God offers the secure consolation of place. But the *reign* of God is more verb than noun. The reign of God offers me the invitation and the challenge of participating in a radically new way of being, a new way of relating to self, to others, and to all of creation. The reign of God is alive, active like yeast, shedding light like a bright lamp, attentive as a bridesmaid, persistent as someone searching for a lost treasure. The reign of God is just and merciful like the foreigner who stops to help; brimming over with forgiveness like the father of a runaway son.

I want to carry the reign of God within me, alive in the innermost aspect of every cell and fiber of my being.

The truth is, most stories of my life are more about touching the reign of God than carrying it deeply within my flesh, my understanding, my attitude. And even the moments of touching the reign of God come not through my willing or my doing, but through God's grace and mercy and endless offers of a second try.

I yearn to do better than merely touch the reign of God. In a few privileged moments of prayer I believe I have glimpsed the reign of God revealed, as Jesus so ardently prayed on the night before he died. More often, I find myself merely touching the fringe of the garment of God's mercy, love, and peace.

Touching the Reign of God is one person's reflection on God's grace at work in life experience. My *being*, my *doing*, and my *reflecting* on my experience: Every one of these elements in the life of mature Christian faith is integral to the reign of God which I, like you, have been uniquely gifted and sent to reveal.

The reflections offered here present one person's imperfect but steadfast attempts to link a Christian way of *being* and a Christian way of *doing* with a Christ-mindful *reflection* on experience, in order to reveal the good news of salvation yet one more time. Like the young and pregnant Mary, my whole being is compelled to proclaim the greatness of the Lord.

These reflections reveal the ongoing search for God's fingerprints on one person's lived experience, an honest search full of wrestling and hopefulness for the grace embedded in human experience, measured to the words of Scripture.

The Christian community lives an incarnational life, divinity enfleshed within humanity. The wisdom we gain from reflecting upon our life experiences affirms again and again that the reign of God does not just appear; it comes about in very particular ways: The blind see, the lame leap; those in bondage are set free. Less dramatically in our day-to-day experience, the hungry are fed, the naked are clothed, the homeless are sheltered, those sick or imprisoned are visited and encouraged, and the thirsty are given refreshment in Jesus' name.

As proclaimers of the living Gospel we will witness the unfolding and outspreading of the reign of God, as people in their particular poverties receive from us—anointed to humbly stand in Jesus' place—those things that they need to be healed and restored here and now. Our living and proclaiming the Gospel is not general but particular, enfleshed and incarnational, because the people whose lives we touch are particular, enfleshed, incarnate, and precious in the eyes of God.

Being, doing, and reflecting on God's work in our lives is not some esoteric process available to the specially trained few. It is a disciplined activity with a name—theological reflection, an activity that is directed and rendered fruitful by the Holy

Spirit within every baptized person. Being, doing, and reflecting on God's work in our lives is a "disciplined" activity because it effectively forms us as disciples of the Lord. As we adhere to this work of being, doing, and reflecting on God's work in our lives we will begin to actually look different, because we will begin to participate more deeply, more truly, more faithfully in our life in Christ—the only authentic life we have.

Study questions for personal or group reflection, offered at the end of each essay, provide direct entry into the process of theological reflection. Use these questions creatively to awaken your imagination, to call forth hidden insight, and to discern God's direction for your life.

Wondrously, as we adhere together to this work of being, doing, and reflecting on God's work in our lives, our world will begin to look different; those whose lives we touch will begin to look different. We can count on this, because it is the work of the Holy Spirit in the body of Christ, the reign of God breaking through everywhere.

List of Abbreviations

Hebrew Scriptures

Genesis	Gen	Psalms	Ps
Exodus	Exod	Jeremiah	Jer
Leviticus	Lev	Ezekiel	Ezek
Deuteronomy	Deut	Zechariah	Zech
Second Samuel	2 Sam		

Apocrypha

Sirach	Sir

Christian Scriptures

Matthew	Matt	Galatians	Gal
Mark	Mark	Ephesians	Eph
Luke	Luke	Philippians	Phil
John	John	Colossians	Col
Romans	Rom	Hebrews	Heb
First Corinthians	1 Cor	First Peter	1 Pet
		First John	1 John
Second Corinthians	2 Cor		

Throw Open the Door of Your Heart

A Spiritual Challenge of John Paul II

AT THE late Pope John Paul's inaugural Mass in October 1978, the new pontiff spoke a challenge to Christians everywhere: *Throw open the door of your heart to Christ.* One person familiar with the Italian language, the language in which the Holy Father spoke, noted that the phrase he used translates literally as: Break the door of your heart off the hinges.

Not "remove the door from its hinges," a gentler phrase suggesting that the door might eventually be rehinged. No, he says: "Break the door off its hinges," suggesting that replacing the door might be a great bother. "Break off the door of your heart and hurl it away," the Holy Father might have said.

DOORS

I like doors. They serve a useful function in my life. I use doors to shut out the world when it's time to go inward. In my office, at noon, I step away from my work, go into a quiet room, close the door, and pray. I do not really leave the world behind because the subject of my prayer is the world, especially those who are in harm's way and who need God's protection and care. So the world is very much with me in my prayer. But it helps to close the door.

At the end of the day I go home, close the door of my apartment, set down my bags, prepare for Evening Prayer, and again I pray. Doors, for me, separate the inner chamber from the outer world.

But John Paul speaks of "the door of your heart," the door behind which I might hide when Christ inconveniently knocks, asking me to open the door not when I deem it is time to encounter him but when he deems it is time for me to encounter him. John Paul is not saying "Answer the door of your heart when Christ knocks." He is saying, "Get rid of the door." In other words: Make it unnecessary for Christ even to knock and to wait for your reply.

CHRIST ON THE OUTSIDE, CHRIST WITHIN

Christ dwelling within me has been a lifelong consolation, a strength to me especially in times of aloneness and spiritual loneliness. I have never doubted Christ's dwelling in me, not even in the darkest of times when I had lost my way. Christ dwelling in me is the easy part.

It's Christ on the outside that challenges me. My heartfelt prayer, "Dwell in me," can easily trail a subtext: "as I imagine you," or "as I understand you to be." Christ on the outside, however, the Christ who knocks at my door at the most inconvenient times, in the most unappealing guises, that's the one who catches me off guard. Christ cleverly disguised as a grumpy store clerk; Christ cleverly disguised as a toothless, unshaven beggar; Christ cleverly disguised as an angry and hurtful youth. Christ everywhere, knocking at the door of my heart.

THE DOOR AS FILTER

It's at times like these, when Christ the unappealing one, Christ the unlovely one, comes knocking at the door of my heart, when

I mistakenly feel grateful for the door. "I am just not available at the moment," I pretend. Or perhaps, "I can't see you, what with the door closed and all. Perhaps later, when I'm ready to be mindful of your needs."

So the door to my heart becomes a handy filtering device. I can filter out the many unexpected presences of Christ, claiming that they can't really *be* Christ. In fact, I quickly filter out these people because obviously they *need* Christ. When they finally *get* Christ, then they can come back and I'll find a place for them in my heart.

I discover, much to my surprise, that my heart looks like a country club, a place of privilege for members only, safe from the noise and smell and disorder of the riffraff. But surely a private club is not what Christ has in mind for his dwelling place.

HURL IT AWAY

John Paul's challenge to break the door of the heart off its hinges can be terrifying. This unhinging of the door of my heart, hurling the door away, suggests that Christ would have the freedom to pass in and out of my heart as he wishes. And why am I startled, in a clutching, self-protective way, at the thought that Christ should enjoy such freedom with regard to my heart? To enter at will, whether it's convenient or inconvenient to me?

It is not just anyone who wants unrestricted access to my heart, but Christ, the One who lived and died, lovingly for my sake and equally for the sake of the world; the One who spared nothing, who would do anything, *anything*, to fulfill his Father's heart's desire that all humankind, all creation, enjoy the one eternal divine embrace. It is this One, the obedient One, the ever-faithful One, who wants unrestricted access to my heart.

ST. PAUL'S INSISTENCE

I should not be startled at the prospect of Christ just walking, unannounced, into my heart. St. Paul has written tirelessly about such a prospect and the utter rightness of it. His words are not mere poetry, but an insistent expression of the mystery into which I have been baptized. "But God proves his love for us," he writes, "in that while we were still sinners Christ died for us" (Rom 5:8).

Christ, thank God, did not wait until I got my life acceptably together before entering into it in an utterly redeeming, transforming way. From all eternity the Father has designed that my life "be conformed to the image of his Son" (Rom 8:29). Do I have a right to subject Christ to the inhospitable formality of knocking at the door of my heart, the Lord of life seeking permission from me to enter what he first has lovingly fashioned and mercifully redeemed?

"We do not live to ourselves," St. Paul writes, "and we do not die to ourselves. If we live, we live to the Lord, and if we die, we die to the Lord; so then, whether we live or whether we die, we are the Lord's" (Rom 14:7–8).

And if I understand the words of the Psalmist, then the Lord's dwelling place, which I take to be my heart by virtue of my baptism into him, is lovely (see Ps 84:1). Wherever he chooses to dwell is lovely because his lovely presence changes everything, restores everything, renews everything.

So why would I need—or even want—a door at the entryway to my heart?

IMAGINE A HEART WITHOUT A DOOR

It may seem odd, or confusing, to say that Christ dwells within the heart but Christ also approaches the heart. Is he here? or is he not yet here? In fact, he is both here, abiding in the heart, and approaching, seeking welcome, shelter, refreshment, understanding, support.

So if I take away the door to my heart, I experience Christ encountering Christ, Christ both giving and receiving. And I am present to provide the space, the setting for this encounter, to look on, yes, and also to participate in the encounter. Christ meeting Christ in my heart is a profound and holy experience of being fully humanly alive, fully engaged in my baptismal life.

Having a heart without a door does not mean that my life must be lived publicly at all times. Having a heart without a door means that in those times when I am called upon to be present to another in the circumstances of life, I am available to what God might have in mind within this encounter. It means that my mind and my imagination are available to the movement of the Holy Spirit in this moment, whether convenient or inconvenient. And my heart anticipates both the desire of the Beloved One and the need of the Wounded One.

Christ meets Christ. Did not Jesus anticipate and long for just such encounter in his heartfelt prayer to his Father on the night before he died, "that they may all be one. As you, Father, are in me and I am in you, may they also be in us, so that the world may believe that you have sent me" (John 17:21).

Touching the reign of God in my life . . .

- In the recent past, when someone has inconveniently knocked at the door of my heart, what have I done in response? How would I describe that encounter? What happened for that person? What happened for me? How was the reign of God more fully revealed—or not revealed—in that situation? What might I do differently the next time?

- Considering these encounters, how—or to what action— might God be calling me in the future?

- Where does all of this fit with my understanding of what God desires for my life?

- What Scriptures or teachings of my Christian heritage shed light or offer me a meaningful way to reflect on this and similar encounters?

- What are some key words, images, phrases, feelings, or expressions of prayer that come forward for me at this time?

2

Your Redeeming Love

W HEN MY phone rang at work that May morning, I was surprised to hear Fred's voice. I had not heard from him in quite a while. Immediately I sensed that something was wrong. He sounded vague and shaky.

"I was thinking maybe we could meet after work one evening this week," Fred said in a thin, raspy voice.

"Of course we can," I replied. I paused. "Fred," I said slowly and clearly, "how are you doing?" I leaned hard into the receiver, hoping I could really hear what was going on with him.

"I had brain surgery ten days ago," he said. There was a long pause. "They took out a chunk of my brain." He paused again. "It's so amazing," he whispered.

A year earlier the doctors had removed a malignant tumor from Fred's back—"a real hockey puck," he had called it. For Fred, I sensed, death had become an unexpected but very real companion. He was only 52.

We met two days later, after work, at a nearby pizza pub. Fred, who was tall and thin and bony to begin with, looked even more gaunt. He moved as though he had only a tentative right to be alive. His skin and hair and eyes looked dull, revealing a numbed spirit within. As we settled into a booth I realized that I was looking at a broken man who now lived with a mystery inside his body, the mystery of a mortal self in search of hope. Fred, who had nurtured an eclectic, coreless spirituality, was now confronted with the cross, and was plainly searching for God. Our conversation was disjointed. I decided to just be there in comforting silence.

Six months passed, and Fred's life continued to change. The VA rest home was a comfortable place, clean and well-staffed. Fred's room had a huge picture window that looked out across a grassy open space. In the distance, beyond the Columbia River, he could see the West Hills of Portland, where I lived. From recent visits I knew that Fred was close, very close, to knowing the Lord. He was not fighting his cancer, not fighting death. "Fred," I asked, trying to sound hypothetical, "if my brother J. Pat were available, would you like him to come visit you?" J. Pat was a priest. He and Fred had briefly met a time or two. Fred's eyes lit up and a pulse of energy ran through his body. "Oh, yes," he replied. He had liked J. Pat from their first encounter two years earlier. Fred was very much at peace, very ready, I sensed, for the Lord's anointing in baptism and the healing food of Eucharist.

Finally I leaned close to his face and looked intently into his eyes. "Fred," I said, "would you like to be baptized?" As though divinely timed, the cold, dark clouds parted enough to let through a burst of pure brilliant sunlight. Fred sat in his wheelchair beside his bed, bathed in this transfiguring light, and raised his ethereal, bony sculptor's hands upward. "Oh yes," he simply said. The joy in his soul silently flooded outward to meet the morning light.

So on a clear, crisp Veteran's Day in November, four of us—J. Pat, myself, my mother, and her husband Tom—headed north across the I-5 bridge to Vancouver, to visit Fred. Though he barely knew my family, we would be Christian community for him on this very special day.

"Stay here in the hallway," I instructed the others, "while I go in and check on Fred."

"I'll find a vase for the flowers," my mother said. She had brought a dozen white roses, to celebrate Fred's baptism.

As I entered Fred's room I found him washed, dressed, clean-shaven, sitting in his chair beside the window, and completely bathed in sunlight. He looked immersed in serene contemplation. When I knocked and entered, he turned his face toward me, and I saw the glow of one who has gazed upon the face of God.

"Fred," I said softly as I approached him, "would you like to be baptized today?"

Fred looked up into my eyes with a radiant expression on his face. *He has begun his passage,* I thought; *he has yielded to the work of dying.* He was looking at me, yet I knew he was still communing with God, or perhaps communing with me from some deep place within the heart of God. I was stunned by the serene beauty in his face.

"Yes, please, yes," Fred whispered, his cool, bony hands reaching upward, ready to receive the gift of eternal life in Christ. His lifetime of unnamed spiritual hunger and longing all became focused in this moment of light, this moment of grace. I took his hands in mine.

"My brother J. Pat is here," I said, "and he can baptize you." J. Pat was prepared, having contacted the chaplain and the local pastor and advised them of Fred's desire.

"Oh please, yes," Fred said, his eyes glistening with readiness and appreciation.

"Wait here," I whispered. I leaned over and kissed him on the cheek, then went out into the hallway.

"He's ready," I said to J. Pat.

"He wants to be baptized today?" my mother asked, vase of white roses in hand. She seemed surprised that this moment of salvation was about to begin, and that she would be a witness to it.

"That's what the roses are for, aren't they?" I replied with a quizzical smile. Her eyes misted up.

"I need a few minutes alone with Fred," J. Pat said. "Then I will ask you all to come in."

For four years—since I had first met Fred—I had hoped for this day, when Fred would let go of his lonely spiritual wanderings and come into the community of the Beloved. In just a few minutes he would make his profession of faith, enter the Christian community, and become part of the body of Christ.

"You can come in now," J. Pat quietly said as he opened the door to the room. We arranged ourselves around the bed. Fred sat in his chair between the picture window and the bed, and I sat on the edge of the bed, opposite him. He extended one arm across the bed, and I reached over and held his hand. His other hand was raised, as though he were ready to receive an invisible, precious, and long-sought gift.

Midway through the rite of baptism, J. Pat addressed me. "Mary Sharon, will you be Fred's godmother?"

The question caught me by surprise. I had never been anyone's godmother, much less godmother to a man living with cancer, a friend preparing to die.

"Yes, I will," I said. Pride and joy and sadness and an overwhelming sense of unworthiness welled up from my heart and lodged in my throat. Fred turned and looked at me with love in his eyes. *Will I be guiding him,* I wondered, *or will he be guiding me, in the days and weeks ahead?* J. Pat poured a small amount of water on Fred's forehead in the threefold manner, and with a towel I caught the glistening water as it mingled with tears of joy tracking down Fred's cheeks.

"Fred, the body of Christ," J. Pat said as he held forth the small white host, and Fred entered into his first sacramental communion with the Lord. *How quietly, how simply, the Lord comes to us,* I thought. *Fred is a new creation in Christ.*

In the following two weeks Fred and I shared amazing conversations, long conversations that lasted two hours or more, when Fred revealed to me some of his conversation with the Lord. His headaches, which had become unbearably severe, unexplainably vanished during our visits. These were his last good days. We both knew it, and we treasured them. He spoke of forgiveness toward those who had hurt him, and healing in his own heart and memories. "Mary Sharon is my godmother," Fred told all of his buddies in B wing. When I knocked, one afternoon, on the door of the V.A. chaplain's office, the chaplain rose from her chair. "You must be Mary Sharon," she said with immediate and genuine warmth, "Fred's godmother."

The dark cold of December came down hard, and Fred's condition went down with it. The headaches became constant, and morphine eroded what little appetite he had left. The hand squeeze of recognition faded away, and now sleep, sometimes troubled sleep, settled in. Fred was slipping away.

On Saturday, December 12th, I went up to the rest home around four in the afternoon. Fred's buddies on B wing were sitting in a circle in the entryway when I arrived, near the doors to the dining room, waiting for supper. "He's resting," one of them said right away. They were keeping a close watch on Fred's condition. They were keeping vigil. "Can you tell him we're thinking about him?" another asked. "Tell him Hal and Spence say they're thinking about him. We're praying for him."

"I will tell him," I replied. I had a hunch they had been waiting all day to let me know how much they cared for their young buddy.

"He has a lot of faith," one of the men said. Another asked, "But how are *you* doing?"

"I'm doing pretty well," I answered.

"Are you keeping the faith?"

"No," I replied with a smile, "I'm spreading it around."

"Keep a little for yourself," he cautioned. I knew he meant it. *Hold some faith in reserve,* he was telling me; *you will need it!*

I walked down the hallway to the end, to Fred's room. I tapped lightly on the door and entered. Fred was neatly tucked into his bed, eyes closed, and perfectly still. I gently took Fred's hand and whispered, "Your buddies Hal and Spence want you to know that they're thinking about you and send you their prayers and good wishes."

Fred squeezed my hand, ever so slightly. That was the last time he showed any recognition of my presence.

I kissed Fred's forehead and walked back down the hall to where the men still sat in a circle. "I gave Fred your good wishes," I said, "and he squeezed my hand in reply. Your caring meant a lot to him."

Early that evening I sat in the dim light of Fred's room. Deep twilight had now faded beyond the West Hills. The hallway light was dimmed, and B wing was settling down for the night. I reflected on Advent, the season of waiting, waiting for the coming of the Lord.

But it is a different coming that I await, I thought, and only by association do I await his coming now. I wait for the Lord to come and take Fred home. Together we await the coming of this One who has known suffering, who has felt the coming of his own death, and who has been raised by the mighty power of his Father's love to new life, endless life in the Father's glory. It is the risen Lord we await in this season of Advent. *The Lord's coming will be personal,* I now understood. *I keep vigil with Fred, keep vigil for the Lord.*

On Sunday, the 13th, the nurse told me that my brother Tim and I were welcome to spend the night in Fred's room. Tim had begun to sit with Fred late in the evenings, a gesture of brotherly love I did not know about. Reminiscing over the Vietnam days had linked them together. "We can wheel in a couple of cots," she offered, "but I doubt he'll die tonight. I think he still has another day in him."

The death rattle had settled in. *This is progress,* I remember thinking, *progress in the work of dying.* There was no going back, no standing in place, only movement forward through this lonely, labored passage. Fred's body struggled to hold on to what thin thread of life still held him here. Now and then he would rub the bad side of his head with the back of his bony wrist as he wrestled, unconscious, with the rampaging monster inside.

On Monday, the 14th, I arrived midmorning again at the rest home. Fred's condition seemed unchanged, though he clearly looked worn out from the battle. He was bathed and clean-shaven, resting in a bed of crisp white sheets.

"This is your going-home day," I whispered in Fred's ear. Fred's hand was porcelain blue-white and cold. "Today we will walk you home to the Lord."

I went out to the phone in the hallway and called Tim, to see if he could sit with Fred in the evening while I went to the home of friends who insisted on offering me respite and feeding me dinner. "I was already planning on spending the evening with him," Tim replied. "It may be pretty close to six by the time I get there."

"Do what you can."

In fact, Tim showed up shortly after five-thirty. We prayed together briefly, and I headed out to wade through evening traffic back across the I-5 bridge and up into the West Hills to my friends' home for dinner.

At first I thought my friend Sarah really did not hear or understand me when I told her that today likely would be Fred's last day. "You come for supper," she had insisted that morning. "Bill will make a fire in the fireplace and I will have soup and salad and bread ready for you. You need it." I did need it. I needed a real meal, and I needed the comfort of friends. *If Fred dies while I am at supper, so be it,* I thought. *The Lord knows how to work things out. Tim is there, so Fred will not die alone.*

After dinner I stopped at the house and pulled some things together so that Tim and I could spend the night with Fred. Along with comforters, pillows, and slippers, I brought my book of poems of Spanish Carmelite mystic St. John of the Cross, as this was his feast day, December 14th, and I wanted to share a poem with Fred.

I got back to the rest home at ten minutes to eleven. The halls were dimmed and quiet. As soon as I walked into the room I noticed the remarkable change in Fred's breathing. The death rattle filled the room. Tim looked at me, tired and deeply sad.

"His breathing has changed," I said.

"No," Tim replied, "he's breathing the same."

"No, Tim, he's not," I said. "I have been away for five hours. I know. His breathing is rapid and shallow and hard. He's struggling."

"Maybe so," Tim conceded.

I took off my coat and gathered my thoughts. "Let's pray," I said. Together we prayed a psalm of Night Prayer and the prayer of commendation of the dying. We knew that the Lord was in the room with us, that we could freely open our hearts in complete trust. Silence and peace came upon the room, even as Fred's breathing rattled on.

I read a poem of John of the Cross, "I Came Into the Unknown," a poem I had chosen at random from the collection. Yet the words were so clearly for Fred, who already had begun his ascent to God.

After I had read the poem, Tim and I each traced the sign of the cross on Fred's forehead, then stepped away from the bed. We began to chat, thinking, I guess, that we had all night to settle in.

But our conversation was cut short. Suddenly, without warning, the labored breathing stopped. It simply . . . stopped. The silence was immediate and huge. The silence that filled the room was complete.

Tim pointed toward the bed. "There he goes," he whispered. I moved immediately to Fred's side and placed my hand on his bony shoulder.

"This is the holy moment, Fred," I said. I was surprised at how strong and clear and full of power my voice was. "This is the moment you have waited for. The Lord is here, Fred. This is the holy moment." I know Fred heard those words as he passed from this earthly life to his life in God.

Fred's head turned away from me to the other side, burning a wide gaze into Tim. Then his head came back to center. His back arched as though his soul were being lifted up from his body. One arm raised upward to rest on his chest, and the other arm slowly, haltingly, followed. And then he came to rest. Fred's dying was complete.

The nurse's assistant prepared the body while Tim and I gathered our things. The little man across the hall, one of Fred's buddies, wheeled out of his room. It was now about eleven-thirty. "How is Fred doing?" he asked with a quiet and genuine concern—perhaps, even, with a knowing.

"Fred died a few minutes ago," I said. The man's eyes and gentle spirit stayed with me, not flinching, not invading my space with emotion. "Fred died peacefully," I told him. "He was surrounded by love."

We talked a little more, and the man returned to his room. A few minutes later he wheeled out of his room again, meeting me in the hallway. He looked at me tenderly. "Peace be with you," he said, his offering of consolation and faith delivered with great loving intention.

"Thank you very much," I said.

"How are you doing," he asked. This was the thoughtful question, the question that Fred's other buddies on B wing had asked me, more than once, over the preceding days.

"I am doing well," I said, offering my words so that he might receive them and draw comfort from them. "Fred died surrounded by love," I said, "and that is the very best way to go."

Before I left the room I came across a notepad I had given Fred, and found these reflections in his shaky handwriting:

> Wed night—M.S. teaches
> Sat—7:00 Mass
>
> Thank you GOD
> for the new friends,
> the fun, the joy.
> Thank you my LORD
> for the good feelings.
>
> To live life
> being reborn.
>
> One day at a time
> Make note about
> thoughts, feelings,
> anxieties.
>
> One step at a time.
> It is in the hands of
> the LORD.
>
> _____
>
> The Father
> The Son
> The Holy Spirit

I'm the material
GOD works on
Clay is the material
I work.

———————————

And what do I say
of LORD, when
the doctors say there
is nothing there.

In the hospital Dr. B. said,
"I cannot heal you."
He let go and let God.

By midnight I was on the road, driving the long lonely stretch of highway across the river and up into the hill in the hounding rain. "O God," I prayed through sheets of rain, "who can understand the path of your redeeming love?"

Touching the reign of God in my life . . .

- What circumstances come to mind in my own experience of a loved one's dying?

- What effect did my presence—or my absence—have on the person who was dying? As I reflect back now, what was that experience for me?

- How was God at work in me and through my presence to the person who was dying?

- How has God opened my heart through experiences of being present to others in their dying? What have these experiences revealed to me of the reign of God?

- What Scriptures or teachings of my Christian heritage shed light or offer a helpful way to reflect on these circumstances?

- What are some key words, images, phrases, feelings, or expressions of prayer that come forward for me at this time?

3

Your Attitude Must Be Christ's

L IVING, AS I do, with the illusion that I know a lot, that I am quite good at what I do, and don't need you to teach me what I obviously do not know, I struggle secretly with what I will call "attitude." It's a weakness I try to hide, especially from myself. I live with a small, persistent fear that others will perceive me as "unteachable," a hallmark of arrogance, a rotten fruit of misguided self-understanding.

I do not want to be perceived as unteachable. In fact, deep down I desire to be teachable, to be formed as a disciple of the Lord. I want to learn what Jesus desires to teach me.

JESUS, TEACHER

If I address Jesus as Teacher, I can expect that he will teach me. If I seek to truly pattern my life on the life of my Teacher, I can expect that what I do will be lost on most people and that in fact my ministry will diminish and be taken away from me, the grain of wheat that dies so that God can reap the harvest. I am quite some distance yet from that level of profound selflessness. In short, if I learn well what my Teacher would teach me, I can expect that my very attitude will be crushed, ground finely, and transformed into something worthy of giving glory to God.

Just before the hymn recalling Jesus' outpouring of self to the point of death, "death on a cross," and his exaltation to the glory of his Father (see Phil 2:6–11), St. Paul delivers a blunt and challenging phrase to the early Christian community. He admonishes, in essence, "Your attitude must be Christ's" (see v. 5). He doesn't add "when it's convenient" or "when you're around people who like you or accept your Christian beliefs." He doesn't say "This is something you might want to work on or strive for." He is not proposing a program of self-improvement but a way of entering wholly, intentionally, unreservedly, into the mystery of God. St. Paul really is writing about intentional *kenosis,* intentional pouring out of one's life lovingly for the benefit of others. Such self-emptying is not an experience I would willingly choose but an experience which God determines, perfectly suited for me in my particular time and circumstance.

The text of Philippians 2 explicitly points to Jesus, actively and intentionally entering into the work of divesting himself of his rightful divine identity, through the human life he assumed and the death-sacrifice he embraced. Though he could have done otherwise, staying comfortably within his divine identity, he emptied himself in loving obedience to his Father's inscrutable and perfect plan. I feel certain that they could have talked it over and come up with a perfectly acceptable but less costly plan. But that's not God's way, and therein lies the mystery.

My understanding of God is that God cannot do something contrary to the divine nature. So some core truth of God—and therefore of human experience—lies embedded in the very nature of this pouring out of self that makes *kenosis* a part of authentic divine—and therefore human—self-expression.

How like God, this self-emptying, and how contrary to that stubborn side of my human nature. The indignation I feel when another driver races to take my turn at a four-way stop is a small but apt example. For all my talk and all my posturing, I can be very much not like Christ. My phoniness is real, but my

Jesus is more real. And it is he whom I choose as my Teacher. I am not the best student, but he is the most excellent Teacher.

THAT CHRIST WOULD HAVE AN ATTITUDE

Attitude, my dictionary tells me, is rooted in the word "aptitude," meaning a fitness or natural ability to accomplish something. Taking that "natural ability" to the physical realm where it gets expressed, attitude means the position or posture one would take to carry out an action or to express a mood, a belief, a conviction.

So if my attitude—or aptitude to express a natural ability—must be Christ's, what attitude could I identify as uniquely his? The hymn in Philippians 2 is instructive:

> Though he was in the form of God,
> Jesus did not regard equality with God
> as something to be exploited. (v. 6)

Though he was in the form of God? But the Triune God—Father, Son, and Holy Spirit—is self-effacing humility poured out in an endless gifting of love. Not *though* Jesus was divine but *because* he was divine, this pouring out of self was not the exception but rather the very core of his divine nature. After all, God could have said "Be redeemed!" and our broken world would have been healed and made right. But God did not work that way, and neither can we.

Precisely because the Son is the enfleshed expression of the Father's mercy, his deepest identity lies in his mission. Mercy, which is the reconciling power of love to restore to wholeness what has been wounded, is not mercy until it is expressed. When you are All Mercy, as God alone is, your being mercy and your doing mercy are one and the same. In God, intention and action work seamlessly together.

"ATTITUDE" TODAY

When someone tells me I have "an attitude," they accurately and painfully point to a certain phoniness, a false superiority, a wall that keeps me—and maybe them, too—from peering into the poverty of my very ordinary life, my finiteness, my mortality. People with "attitude" are not generally perceived as kind, having forgotten—or perhaps never learned—that we are all "of a kind," all part of humankind which God deemed good in creation, and which Jesus dignified, loved, and redeemed in his Incarnation, his death, and his resurrection.

"Your attitude must be Christ's," St. Paul insists. A phony, self-inflated stance in life cannot coexist with the only authentic attitude originating in God and expressed in the person of Jesus Christ. Paul does not say, "Your attitude must be like Christ's." No, he is not urging imitation of, but rather, direct participation in, Christ's attitude which is at once a way of being and a way of doing, lovingly oriented toward the other's good. We participate in Christ's attitude of outpouring of self not for our own good—although such self-humbling does us a world of good—but for the good of humankind. We directly participate in Christ's redemptive work; we intimately share his mission of reconciling the world to his Father, restoring all of humankind to fullness of friendship with God. Our attitude, and therefore our relationships and dealings with others, must somehow touch, participate in, and reveal Christ's redeeming work of dying, rising, and breathing forth new life.

THE CHALLENGE

In our culture today, attitude sells—the edgier, we believe, the better. Attitude can be purchased everywhere. Yet the convenience-driven culture of excess and privilege, of which I am a part, seems cocooned against the light of Jesus' mission of mercy, justice, and redemption. We can protect ourselves from the nasty elements of human life such as pain, responsibility, indebtedness to other human beings, duty to the commonweal, until we hatch forth into misshapen and isolated empty pods. No wonder we have little taste for an attitude such as Christ's. It would expose our world for the empty, upside down place that it is.

When we let it claim us, Christ's attitude turns our distorted world rightside up. That we would feel threatened by the invitation to be restored to friendship with God speaks sadly for a culture that is so privileged. Remember who you are, St. Paul reminds us; you have been purchased, and at what a price!

Touching the reign of God in my life . . .

- What attitudes do friends generally perceive in me? What attitudes do various family members perceive in me? What attitudes do co-workers most often perceive in me?

- How would I describe my attitude toward life as I experience it? My attitude toward my work? How would I describe my attitude toward those I love the most? How would I describe my attitude toward neighbors? co-workers? those who irk me?

- How does my attitude affect family relationships? Workplace relationships? Neighbor relationships?

- What Scriptures or teachings of my Christian heritage shed light or offer a meaningful way to reflect on my attitude toward my life, work, and relationships?

- Does Christ's attitude of self-humbling, loving regard for the other have any actual, observable effect on how I live my life?

- What are some key words, images, phrases, feelings, or expressions of prayer that come forward for me at this time?

4

Listen for the Lord

MY MOST ardent prayer comes in the early hours of morning, before the new day stirs, before the grind and rush of work can touch me. Open-hearted, with every best intention, I come before the Lord, my life open to the movement and work of his holy Spirit.

In the perfect still moment I pray in utter sincerity, "Lord, whatever you would have me hear, let me hear it."

I brace myself for the word of correction, for the admonishing, humbling, even humiliating word. I admit to myself the possibility of a word that will nail my sin and strip away all cover and consolation.

I have learned, over time, to not rush the Lord. Allow him three days, a week, three weeks. Wait on the Lord. I can wait on the Lord, to hear what he would have me hear.

A FIRST WORD

At the end of the lunch break on Saturday, well into the weekend workshop, Gary, who sits in the front row, approaches me. He's one of those people I unfairly tag as someone I don't want to get tangled up with in conversation, one of those people with special issues that they feel compelled to share in great detail over a ten-minute break. I have no real reason to think this. I just do.

So Gary zeroes in. I smile and fix my attention on him.

"I have a message for you," Gary says. He equally fixes his attention on me. "You are very special to God. I need to tell you that."

I open my mouth to say something, but for once words fail me.

"You need to know that you are very special to God," Gary repeats.

"Thank you," I weakly reply.

Sunday evening when the workshop is over and I get back home, I ask the Lord in prayer, "Was that what you wanted me to hear?"

Surely, I am thinking, the Lord must have something more that I should hear, something more challenging than these simple words of love and consolation. Still, I think, who am I to diminish those precious words I received this weekend? *You are very special to God.* Were those words the only answer to my prayer?

I spend a week holding all of this lightly. Like Mary, I ponder these things in my heart. "Lord," I pray again, "what would you have me hear?"

AN UNEXPECTED SECOND WORD

The sky clears suddenly on a Sunday afternoon. I come up for air after two hours of writing, put on my sneakers and my fanny pack, and head out for a four-mile walk.

On my return toward home, a block or two past the Methodist Church and the rest home, I see an old hatchback pull up to the curb. The horn honks a couple of times. A man hollers out the car window to some children playing in the paved yard in back of the school. It's not a friendly-sounding voice, not a friendly-looking car.

The car then pulls into the schoolyard. The man with the unfriendly voice hollers at the tall young girl in the group. His voice sounds commanding in a coarse, coercive way. She tentatively approaches the car, then tentatively moves away. Instinctively I think that what is happening is not good. Now I hear a second man's voice coming from inside the car. The boys on their bikes circle around in the distance. They are too young to be any help, if what's going on is what I think is going on. This girl is being abducted, I wildly imagine.

I slow down, observing the scene as I pass the chain link fence around the schoolyard, peering through as I keep walking. I memorize the look of the car, memorize the numbers on the license plate.

Stop, I tell myself. *Intervene. Something's not right.*

The girl wavers beside the car. The men holler coarsely again. The boys circle aimlessly on their bikes. *Stop,* I tell myself. *Intervene.*

My feet keep walking.

I'm a block away, now two blocks. I cross the tracks, wait at the light on South Washington. *Go back,* I tell myself. *It's not too late.*

My feet keep walking.

"Lord, what would you have me hear?" I recall myself praying. "A honking horn? A nasty-voiced man hollering to a young girl on a playground on a Sunday afternoon?" I am not prepared for this.

My feet keep walking.

"Would you have me hear a car door slam? An engine race as a captor takes his prey?"

My feet keep walking. I could turn back, but I don't. "My sin is ever before me," I recall the Psalmist saying. My sin of refusal to intervene surely is before me now.

I get home, pick up my car keys, and drive back to the schoolyard. More children are there now, hanging out in groups. I park at the curb across the street, turn off the engine, and look for the young girl. I think she was wearing a light blue knit shirt, yes, but I see no light blue shirts among the tight cluster of girls near the dumpster at the far end of the yard.

I get out of the car, walk across the street, enter the school-yard, and slowly approach two girls. Two boys on bikes come in close and circle, the same two who I think were there earlier. I ask them if they saw an old dark red car pull into the yard twenty minutes earlier.

"No," they say. "We just got here."

So I walk across the yard to the far corner where a dozen girls are gathered. I catch the drift of their conversation. I hear them talking about drugs. They fall silent as I approach.

I ask them if they saw the car, or the girl in the light blue shirt. The group is silent. They are sizing me up. One of them says, "Yeah, I saw them."

"Did the girl get into the car?" I ask.

"Yeah." They look at me suspiciously. I do not blame them.

A young boy wheels up on his bike. He had been there earlier. I recognize him.

"Yeah, she got in the car," he says. "She's my girlfriend." His expression drifts into a smile. "Those shoes," he says, rolling his eyes, "she's got those shoes." He must be four years her junior, I think, and smitten by her style.

"Did she know the man in the car?" I ask. I look at all the girls, searching for information. I look at the young boy. "Did she know him?"

"Yeah," one girl says.

"Yeah," the young boy pipes up. He waves an arm vaguely. "He's the dad of one of her friends." His voice tells me that how she knows the man is more complicated than he can explain. The thread of connection seems thin. But no one in the group seems alarmed that she would get into this man's car.

The girls look a little shaken that a stranger has approached them across the schoolyard and is questioning them so closely on the whereabouts of one of their peers. I think they wish I would go away now so they can get back to their conversation.

I turn and walk back across the schoolyard, not convinced of the young girl's safety. I get into my car, knowing that I have something of a vehicle description, the license plate number, and a location and time, should I hear a report on the morning news of a missing girl, or worse, a girl's body found in a ditch.

I head back home, knowing something else, too. Even though I had gone back to check on this troubling situation, I'd kept on walking when everything in me was saying: Stop. Intervene.

"My sin is ever before me," I remember the Psalmist saying. "What is evil in your sight I have done."

Back home, I toss down my car keys, go to my prayer space, and fall on my knees, my spirit crushed. Too clearly I recall my prayer, uttered in all earnestness and now ringing so hollow: "Lord, whatever you would have me hear, let me hear it."

You let me know what needed to be heard, and I did not want to hear it. For you, it wasn't enough that I merely heard something. You wanted more of me—to be your ears, your eyes, yes, and on hearing signs of danger, to stand in your place, to take action, since you could not be there personally.

I asked of you; you answered me. You asked of me, and I walked away. Have mercy on me, Lord. Have mercy on us all.

Touching the reign of God in my life . . .

- When do I experience my most authentic prayer? Is it intentional? Random? What is that prayer like for me?

- In what recent experience has authentic prayer cast a situation in a new light or urged me to respond in an unexpected way?

- How does God seem to be calling me through the content of my prayer? How does God seem to be calling me through the circumstances I encounter? How would I describe the link between my prayer and my life circumstances?

- What Scriptures or teachings of my Christian heritage shed light or offer a meaningful way to reflect on my prayer and the circumstances in my life?

- What are some key words, images, phrases, feelings, or expressions of prayer that come forward for me at this time?

5

No Longer for Ourselves

I MAGE, I finally have come to accept, *is* everything.
I don't mean the distorted lifestyle images that splash across
our TV screens or the image people work hard to project in the
social clubs downtown. That's not the kind of image I accept in
the phrase, "Image is everything."

Yet "accept" is not a passionate enough word. I do not
merely *accept* that image is everything. I *believe*—I take as a
matter of faith strong enough to shape the way I see the world
and live my life—that image is everything. I was made, I read
in the first chapter of Genesis, in the image of God. And you
were made in the image of God. All of humankind and all of
the created order was made in the image of God. And God pro-
nounced us all "very good!"

As the image of God—on my good days, in my best
moments—my very being is an expression of God's delight. On
good days I say the same of you, and of all of creation.

But I am not the center of this world of delight. One
precedes me, the One who is the sacred icon of God, Christ
Jesus who is the living human "image of the invisible God, the
firstborn of all creation" (Col 1:15). He "did not regard equal-
ity with God" as something to be snatched or coveted, St. Paul
tells us, but rather, he "emptied himself, taking the form of a
slave," becoming "obedient to the point of death—even death
on a cross" (Phil 2:6ff.).

This is the image of God I often would rather not look at. It wasn't Jesus' wit or charm or talent that made him the image of God but his obedience, even to the point of an unjust and early death. Selfless obedience and radical dependence on God are the image in which I am destined to be spiritually formed. Did I understand this when I agreed to a Christian way of life?

Jesus had serious work to do, reconciling all of humankind and all of creation to God, restoring human dignity by restoring that divine image in the soul of every living being, in the very soul of the world.

So it follows that you and I also have serious work to do, not separate from or in addition to Jesus' work of redemption, but work that directly participates in that very selfless, loving act of redemption, restoring within the human community and in creation the dignity and beauty and worthy delight of our divine origins.

I find a core message of prophetic urgency in St. Paul's insistence: *We live no longer for ourselves but for him who died for us and was raised again* (see 2 Cor 5:15). For me this truth is a deeply held conviction, one I must speak boldly and often.

But what would my life look like if I truly embraced this injunction to live no longer for myself? What would our world look like if all Christian men and women lived no longer for themselves but for him who died for us and was raised again?

BE LIKE GOD

I like to think that I have learned how to live a life centered in Christ. And then the Teacher comes along with a quiz: "How much love do you have?" Or he offers me a test: "Can you look into the face, the eyes, of this person who lives in the margins and find Me?" My scores are inconsistent, and I am sure that the Teacher is not convinced that I have learned the lesson.

And what is the lesson? It is an evocative challenge: Be like God. "Return to your original state of being," my Teacher might say. "Be what you were meant to be, the image of God" (see Gen 1:27).

The Hebrew and Christian Scriptures offer me several images of God: all-powerful, all-knowing, all that I never will be. But in the Wisdom literature of the Apocrypha a lovely little phrase is tucked in amid admonitions against those who would seek vengeance on their enemies: Remember the covenant of the Most High, and forgive faults (see Sir 28:7). *Be like God.*

Indeed, be like God, not by being all-powerful or all-knowing, but by being, quite simply, forgiving. I might say "all-forgiving," because God does not forgive in half-measures. It is sometimes easier to pretend at being all-powerful or all-knowing than to be all-forgiving, or even forgiving of just one person, the one who most distresses me on this particular day, in this particular moment.

What was the time-honored covenant between God and the Israelites—and by extension, the new covenant in Christ Jesus with all of humankind? "I will be your God, and you will be my people" (Lev 26:12). It was a covenant of love and generous provision, requiring obedient faithfulness (see 26:3ff.). *We will be in extraordinary relationship,* God was saying. These covenant words appear again in the book of the prophet Ezekiel, when the Israelites had profaned God's name among the nations. "I will gather you back and give you a fresh start, giving you a new heart and a new spirit," God says through his prophet; "you shall be my people, and I will be your God" (see Ezek 36:22–28). *Together we will be in extraordinary relationship.*

Again, in the book of the prophet Zechariah, God renews the covenant, speaking with a jealous and fiercely protective love: "They shall be my people and I will be their God in faithfulness and righteousness" (Zech 8:8).

Who am I, and who are we, riddled as we are with unfaithfulness and selfish pursuits, to be included in God's covenant love? If God only knew how lukewarm my heart can be in the inconvenient circumstance, or how divided my heart really is in my dealings with people who annoy me. But God does know, and that's the point. To be in covenant relationship with God is to be everlastingly joined in love to One whose eternal embrace I am supremely unworthy to enjoy. In the Gospel of Luke, Elizabeth captured something of this awe-filled unworthiness when she said to young, pregnant Mary: "But why has this happened to me, that the mother of my Lord comes to me?" (Luke 1:43).

God does know how "unlike God" I can be. But the evocative challenge remains: *Be like God*. Remember the covenant of the Most High, and forgive faults. If I want to be "like God," my assignment is clear: I must forgive faults. In the challenge, God evokes the original divine image emblazoned in my soul, an image which I am not privileged to see, an image blazing with divine passion which in my small-hearted ways I have tried to hide from God.

BE LIKE CHRIST JESUS

In the Christian view of things, to "live for oneself" is nonsense. Jesus insisted on servant-heartedness in his disciples, and showed us what that looks like in his living and in his dying. Much in contemporary American culture would contradict that servant-hearted way of life with the ever-present lure of the many little indulgences that make us think that living for ourselves is a good thing, and actually necessary.

Being like Christ Jesus has never held the promise of the easy or convenient way. Being like Christ Jesus is countercultural; it goes against the grain. To some it's downright laughable.

So if "living for oneself" is nonsense to a Christian, then what way of living does make sense? It is a way of living that gets our focus off of how others are living—and the lifestyles to which we should aspire—and keeps us centered in the Lord. For none of us lives for oneself alone, St. Paul insists, and none of us dies for oneself alone. For "if we live, we live to the Lord, and if we die, we die to the Lord; so then, whether we live or whether we die, we are the Lord's" (see Rom 14:7–8). St. Paul leaves no room for ambiguity.

Living no longer for ourselves is not one option among many for Christians, because we have been baptized into Christ Jesus who knew only how to live for his Father. He knew only how to live lovingly for the sake of the world which his Father so loved (see John 3:16). Jesus' life was an oblation of love, a pouring out of love, because selfless outpouring of love is what God does best, and it is what we do because we are made in the image and likeness of God.

To be like Christ Jesus means that my life too is designed to be an oblation of love, a selfless outpouring of love, in obedience to the Father for the sake of the world. My life lived as an oblation of love teaches me and forms me, conforming me to Christ, a formation full of inconvenience and self-surrender, a formation that gives shape and meaning to my life.

To be like Christ Jesus means, too, that in some way I will participate in the witness of his nail scars. In the upper room, insisting that he see the risen Lord for himself, Thomas spoke a deep conviction, saying in essence: If the one whom I follow cannot show me the mark of the nails in his hands and the wound in his side, he is not worth following, not worthy of my belief (see John 20:24–25). If I think I can get through this life unscarred in the service of love, I am sorely mistaken.

To be like Christ Jesus means that I must step forward to share in the priestly role of Christ who intercedes before his

Father for the sake of the world. When I pray as Christ prays for the sake of those who need God's mercy and healing, God's protection and providence, I face a risk. Do I want to be touched by others' poverty or pain or discouragement? Do I want to enter through the door of empathy into others' dark caverns of loss and addiction and humiliation and despair? My share in Christ's priestly mission requires that I go with him, faithfully, willingly, lovingly, into those caverns of human anguish, so that his grace can be more fully unleashed to penetrate the cold and stony terrain of human experience.

St. Paul is right: We live no longer for ourselves but for him who died and was raised. My outpouring of self in Jesus' name is a fruit of my baptism, just as Jesus' self-offering was a fruit of his baptism. Every outpouring of self in Jesus' name is a significant step in the maturing of Christian faith.

BE MERCY POURED OUT FOR THE WORLD

"Lord, how many times shall I forgive my brother when he sins against me?" Peter asks (see Matt 18:21). It is an honest question from a man who earnestly seeks to follow his Lord and to be like him. It is a "quantity" question, though, to which Jesus gives a "quality" answer: You must forgive your brother, or your sister, *from your heart* (see v. 35).

So we come back to forgiveness. What do we know of God? God is the One who forgives. Our life's work is to be like God, so Jesus' answer to Peter's question on forgiveness is instructive for us as well. I try to imagine a God who would withhold forgiveness, as posed in the Psalmist's question: If you, O Lord, should mark iniquities, O Lord, who could stand? *But in you we find forgiveness* (see Ps 130:3f.).

What could I say to such a God who would keep a record of my sins and withhold forgiveness from me? Or what could

I say to a God who thought forgiveness of sin wasn't all that important? Would such a God say to me, "Oh, it was nothing"? My very discomfort with such a response would be the Holy Spirit agitating and crying out on my behalf.

And reconciliation is exactly what I seek from God when I have sinned. I seek that aspect of divine love that restores me to right relationship with God, with myself, and with those I have harmed by my sin. In the grace of reconciling, God's mercy restores my inherent dignity and brings me back to life in the human community. God's mercy is as necessary for my life as the air I breathe. Deprived of God's mercy, I would die and truly be dead.

Jesus teaches us, and shows us by his life, by the works of his public ministry, and by his suffering and death, how to be God's mercy enfleshed and poured out. As Christians we are impelled to go beyond mere words of forgiveness. In every aspect of our being we are urged to courageously identify more deeply with Jesus, bringing those who are wounded and incapacitated by sin before God in prayer, and interceding for God's compassion and mercy.

Now and then I wonder: How much must I give in this Christian way of life? The answer comes, sure and distinct: All. God asks for all.

And what do I receive in return? Again the answer comes, sure and distinct: All. God settles for nothing less.

Touching the reign of God in my life . . .

- In my life, where do I find the invitation—or challenge—to be "like God"? How does that invitation or challenge specifically shape my actions, my attitude, my presence?

- In what situations do I find myself trying to be "like Christ Jesus"? What is that experience for me? What are the specific, immediate outcomes? What are some specific longer-term outcomes?

- When, recently, was I able to genuinely forgive someone? How would I describe that work of forgiving? What other work of forgiving remains for me to do?

- What Scriptures or teachings of my Christian heritage offer me encouragement in the work of forgiving?

- What are some key words, images, phrases, feelings, or expressions of prayer that come forward for me at this time?

6

Coming Up Short

I EASILY delude myself. I like to think that I live a life that is open to God, open to the movement of the Holy Spirit. But how quickly walls of resistance go up when circumstances insist that I look someone in the eye and speak the humbling phrase: *I was wrong; I am sorry. Please forgive me.* In fact, the dust and bones of past relationships attest to my resistance to admitting my faults. Humility, never my strong suit, is a virtue for which I have chosen not to pray.

Equally challenging for me are the words: *I forgive you,* words that suggest that we are in relationship enough for me to feel hurt by something you have done. But I hold no claim against you. I set you free.

Forgiveness seems unfair to the one doing the forgiving. The aggrieved one does not collect payback, but seems to come up short—in fact, considers coming up short as fair. By human standards, only fools settle for coming up short.

JESUS' MISSION: RECONCILING US TO THE FATHER

At the start of his public ministry, Jesus held the crowds spell-bound, because he taught "with authority" (see Mark 1:22, 27). This most excellent Teacher did not merely transmit words carefully learned from earlier teachers; rather, he spoke with the power of the Word of God, the Word which he was, in the Father, before the beginning of the world (see John 1:1–5). He taught powerfully with words because his actions, his life, already carried the indisputable power and authority of God. His entire public ministry was oriented toward that fateful journey to Jerusalem where the Teacher became both High Priest and perfect sacrifice of reconciling love, once, and for all. Gathering all of humankind into the reconciling embrace of his crucifixion, Jesus made of our sinful mess a perfect and pleasing offering to his Father.

St. Paul tells us that God has reconciled us to himself through Christ Jesus (see 2 Cor 5:18), the Son of God serving as mediator.

And Christ Jesus was no ordinary mediator.

To mediate means to step into the gap, to serve as a connector for two disconnected parties, to intervene between one side and the other so that the two, who have fallen out of harmony, can return to harmony. Mediators carry messages from one side to the other, perhaps earnestly desiring a good outcome, but not really having to pay personally to reconcile the differences.

But Jesus placed his life personally in the gap. "Take and eat; this is my body," he says to his disciples, "take and drink the cup of my blood, the blood of the new and everlasting covenant, poured out for the forgiveness of sins" (see Mark 14:22–24). He handed over his flesh, his body, his life, still young and full of promise, rather than back down from his mission of bringing about the new creation. While we were still sinners, St. Paul reminds us—not after we had reformed and repented, not after we had gotten over our sinful, mean-spirited ways—but *while we were still sinners,* Jesus made the supreme sacrificial offering of his life, restoring us to blessed friendship with his Father (see Rom 5:8). Our reconciliation is personal.

When Jesus forgives me, he has already taken my sin—raw, ugly, and inexcusable—and has stood, in my place, before the throne of God. "Father," I hear him say, "these despicable things *I* have done, and these things required of me, by the love you have shown me, *I* have failed to do. What is shameful in your eyes, what is loathsome and heartbreaking to you, Father, I have done." And as Jesus says these things to his Father, I imagine him shielding me behind him, giving no hint that the wrongdoing he unjustly bears really is mine. He who did not know sin became sin for our sake, St. Paul writes, so that against all logic and defying the norms of justice, "we might become the righteousness of God" (2 Cor 5:21).

MY ROLE IN THE WORK OF RECONCILIATION

One thing that I will finally grasp, I am sure, when I die and enter into God's presence will be a clear understanding that all along my Christian journey I was called not merely to follow Christ Jesus but to be in intimate, one-flesh relationship with him. By God's grace and mercy I share already in the divinity of Christ who has humbled himself to share in my sin-riddled humanity. He is pleased to claim me as his own for reasons I cannot fully fathom this side of eternity. I trust his pledge of unconditional love as though my life depended on it, because, in truth, it does. "For you were bought with a price," St. Paul writes (1 Cor 6:20; see also 7:23). The price of my soul is the blood of the Lamb of God.

If I have been purchased by the blood of the Lamb and now am enfleshed in Christ who reconciles, then my work also, which really is his work, is to reconcile. If his work of mercy is to restore humankind and all of creation to right relationship with the Father, then my work of mercy is to restore those whose lives I touch to right relationship with the Triune God. In baptism

I have been appointed to stand in the place of Christ Jesus, his reconciling presence embedded and radiating forth in my flesh, my spirit, my words and tone of voice, my gestures, the look in my eyes.

In those rare, spiritually lucid moments, at some level I understand this and by the grace of God transcend myself to enter into this work of reconciliation. In those rare, spiritually lucid moments I intentionally participate in the priesthood of Christ, extended to me in baptism, and plead with Christ, in the Holy Spirit, before the throne of the Father for that outpouring of mercy that reconciles a hurting world, in this place and time, to the heart of God.

On those less focused days, when I find myself entangled in my own brokenness or the brokenness of others, I struggle to remember that I am called to reveal Christ's presence, even in the unlovely moments. Often that call to reveal Christ means "clinging to nothing," letting go my rightful claim to be heard, to be understood, to be justified, excused, or forgiven. For as much as I want to live a life that is intentionally open to God, I seldom am eager to pay the price in my own flesh and spirit on behalf of those who challenge me, persecute me, or merely rub me the wrong way. Far from selfless, I find every reason to justify my self-righteousness. I do not like to come up short.

And neither did Jesus. On the night before he died he prayed to his Father that the bitter cup of death would be removed from him, yet whatever pleased his Father, that alone was what he wanted to do. I too pray for strength of spirit to fulfill my priestly role in Christ, of which I feel so unworthy. And I pray for the courage to gladly come up short for the sake of others, if it means that in some small way others can touch the reign of God through me.

Touching the reign of God in my life . . .

- In the recent past, what are some instances when I have come up short or was denied what was rightfully mine? What was the injustice there?

- In the recent past, have I mediated between two parties where injustice, perceived injustice, or irreconcilable viewpoints put a wedge in the relationship? What was that mediator role for me? What insights did I gain from that experience?

- How does this notion of sharing in the priesthood of Christ touch my life? Do I feel as though I share in the priesthood of Christ when I pray for others and for the world? If I were to intentionally embrace this role, how might my prayer be different? What else in my life might change?

- What Scriptures or teachings of my Christian heritage shed light or offer a meaningful way to reflect on my share in the priesthood of Christ?

- What are some key words, images, phrases, feelings, or expressions of prayer that come forward for me at this time?

7

Let Me See Your Face

I T'S EARLY Christmas morning. Outside the world is still, and all within my heart and my home is at peace. The starry pre-dawn crackles with winter cold, while the walls of my prayer room dance in warm flickering candlelight.

I have awaited this Christmas morning with extraordinary joy, because today I will act on a long-held desire. I will serve Christmas dinner at Brother André's Café in downtown Portland. As I anticipate the experience in this quiet hour before dawn, I am drawn to Psalm 27:

> "Come," my heart says, "seek his face!"
> Your face, Lord, do I seek.
> Do not hide your face from me. (vv. 8–9)

Yes! On this day when the world celebrates God's enfleshed entry into human history, I want to see the face of the Lord in the faces of those whom I will serve today, people whose lives and stories are very different from mine, whose faces are etched with struggles I have never known.

NOON

Brenda from my church comes by to pick me up. The back of her minivan is packed tight with pies, blankets, men's and women's coats and winter clothing. She is well familiar with the network of social service agencies downtown, and I'm grateful that she is taking me under her wing for the Christmas dinner. I'm way out of my comfort zone, stepping into a part of my world that feels foreign and overwhelming to me.

My job, Brenda tells me, is to be a hostess, to greet people when they come in, get them seated at a table, get them coffee or juice, and make them feel at home until their meal is served.

I can do that, I think to myself. No problem. I'll just unleash my cheery personality and weave the warmth among the tables of dinner guests. A team of us from the parish will be there, hosting and serving meals and helping out in other ways.

As the minivan winds its way into the old section of downtown, I sit back, close my eyes, and savor this part of my Christmas celebration. I imagine the people whom I will meet, imagine their faces, the gleam in their eyes, the cold, rough hands, the warming hearts, one more expression of human community. Yes, this is the celebration of Christmas which I have long anticipated, before me at last.

We pull up to the dining hall and quickly unload the van. Helpers come out to whisk the pies and clothing into the hall. Brenda pulls up around the block, parks, and we enter the dining hall together. The world I am entering feels daunting to me, yet my heart is fortified by that phrase that has lingered since dawn: "Your face, Lord, do I seek. Do not hide your face from me."

Inside, I put on my apron and name badge, and duck into the kitchen for some instruction on hostess duties. I'm ready to go. Everyone is so kind. A complete stranger, I feel folded, unconditionally, into a community that knows no strangers.

LATE AFTERNOON

Back at home, I have half an hour to freshen up and get to my own family celebration of Christmas. But I am numbed, shocked, unable to get beyond waves of anguish at what I have experienced today. I resist even looking at my prayer space because I know that if I go near it, I will cry uncontrollably. My prayer was answered, all right, and I did not measure up. I am crushed by the complete poverty of my prayer, and shaken by the face of the Lord when he did at last appear.

Out of the corner of my eye, in the midst of conversation and all of the dining hall commotion, I became aware of a very tall, very large man who had entered the room. Dressed against the winter chill, his massive frame filled the doorway. Out of the corner of my eye I saw that he stood alone, unmoving. No one came near him. He seemed a giant of a man.

I turned to look at him directly, unprepared for what I saw.

The skin on his face, unmoving and devoid of expression, was a translucent porcelain pink. Small metal clamps, like those clamps the dry cleaner uses to pin my skirts to their hangers, fastened this fragile skin to his scalp and to the folds of flesh around his neck and throat. His eyes appeared as two little red coals sunken deep within the puffy flesh. I froze in place while my soul howled forth in anguished horror.

As he looked toward me, then through me, I realized that I could not move toward him, nor could I turn away. My limbs and joints were locked in a paralysis of shock and horror and, yes, revulsion.

A guest approached me with a question, and I gladly welcomed the diversion. I turned from the man with the stapled pink skin and coal-red eyes and answered her. We talked some, and then I poured my attention onto the people at the table nearest me. "More coffee? Pie?" I asked, hoping for takers. "How was the meal?" I asked, hoping to dissolve my horror with simple conversation.

I went to the next table, helped a couple up from their seats, made small talk, wished people a merry Christmas, thanked them for coming.

Keep talking, I thought to myself. *Keep moving. Do not turn around. Someone else will welcome that man. He'll find his way. I don't need to be the one to greet him. He'll be just fine.*

I straightened up and turned, just enough to see if the man with the stapled pink skin and coal-red eyes was still in the room. Cautiously I scanned one small portion of the room, and then the next, hoping to catch him only peripherally. Strangely, I did not want him to leave, yet I knew that eye contact with him would oblige me to acknowledge him, approach him, engage him in the warmth of the celebration, just as I had done with every other guest.

By now the crowd had started to thin. In the kitchen the dishwasher lunged and steamed at full force, while clean-up crews cleared tables, working respectfully around the edges of lingering conversations.

In the corner of my eye I saw him, the man with the painful face, the man who stood apart and alone. Thankfully a woman from my church was with him now, striking up a conversation with him as though they were old friends. Maybe she knew him; maybe he was one of the café regulars until some calamity befell him, perhaps a flash fire. Maybe she knew what he had gone through. She talked easily to him, using words of encouragement like a balm to relieve his discomfort.

A wave of gratitude washed through me—not because someone else had stepped up to do what I could not do, but because the man with the painful face, the man with the coal-red eyes, the giant of a man who stood apart and alone was welcomed into the circle of warmth and friendship on this day of the Incarnation.

You favored me, my Lord; you answered my prayer. I asked to see your face today, my Lord, and you revealed it. It *was* your face. It was *your* face. You stood near me and I backed away.

And now I remember your words to the rich young man who observed the law yet sought something more: "You are not far from the reign of God," you told him with great love. But "not far" is not close enough for you.

Touching the reign of God in my life . . .

- What are some things I have prayed for, in recent weeks or months or years, for my life (such as someone to love, patience, guidance in work or family situations, resolution regarding a particular circumstance)? How has God answered my prayers?

- What circumstances come to mind in which my prayer has been answered in unexpected, challenging, and perhaps unsettling ways? How have those experiences shaped the way I pray now?

- In what ways does the Lord "reveal his face" in painful or challenging situations in my life? How does he reveal his face in people I would rather not encounter?

- What Scriptures or teachings of my Christian heritage shed light or offer a meaningful way to reflect on these circumstances?

- What are some key words, images, phrases, feelings, or expressions of prayer that come forward for me at this time?

8

Meditation on Three Words

I DO not have a cell phone. I gave away my TV. I live, at the moment, in a land of few people scattered broadly across howling open spaces. I live alone, in the heart of solitude. And oftentimes, in prayer, I simply grow tired of words.

Tired may not be the right word. Sometimes words simply miss the mark for me in prayer, in those moments when the soul transcends any expression which the mind or imagination or even the heart can craft.

AT THE TABLE OF THE DIVINE BANQUET

Words began to fall away some months ago when I first deeply gazed upon Andrei Rublev's early 15th century icon of the Holy Trinity. I was captivated by the serene communion of Son with Father, of Father with the Holy Spirit, and the loving gaze of the Holy Spirit upon the world. Their presence to one another, their wordless loving gaze, is enough, this sacred icon seems to say. Indeed, their wordless loving gaze, this icon reminds me, is source, soul, and sustenance for all that exists.

I want to be part of this wordless communion, the soul seems to say. *I want it always.* I shall have this wordless loving communion, the soul insists believingly, and nothing shall interrupt this wordless communion.

IN THE DARK SPACE BEFORE DAWN

I pull myself up from sleep, briefly disoriented from the sound of the alarm pulsing staccatolike through the quiet night. I stretch, rise, and minutes later light the candle before this sacred icon of the Holy Trinity. The world outside still sleeps, unaware of the sacred silence into which I enter. Gently I sound the small chime once, twice, a third time, gently as though to awaken the soul from blessed sleep. *Arise, my love,* the chime and the candle and the dark night and the sacred icon seem to say. Arise. A blessed communion awaits you.

Wrapped in the peace of this dark space before dawn I notice my breathing, the breathing, really, of the Holy Spirit within me. Breathing in, the Spirit penetrates the innermost spaces of my being, my bones and the marrow of my bones; penetrates through arteries and veins and the blood vibrantly pulsing within each vein. I breathe out all surrender, all gratitude, all praise, all presence before the One who is desirous and worthy of my total being. Prayer begins to stir.

"Likewise the Spirit helps us in our weakness," I recall from St. Paul's letter to the Romans, "for we do not know how to pray as we ought, but that very Spirit intercedes with sighs too deep for words" (Rom 8:26). I breathe in, and let my breath come out in a sigh. Again I breathe in, and exhale a sigh, this time deeper in tone, coming from a deeper place within. A third time I breathe in, and on the out-breath the perfect word forms, the word which is the name above every name: *Jesus.*

The soul immediately is fully composed in peace, having found that one word which is her home, her safety, her shelter, her food, solid food and blessed nourishment.

Jesus, the soul prays, breath after breath; now no longer an audible sigh but a prayer-word reverently prayed from the interior space of soul.

Jesus, the soul prays, the Word which renders all other words extraneous, noisy, flat.

Jesus, the soul prays, and becomes like a lush watered garden, a fruitful place refreshed by the presence of Love.

Jesus, the soul prays, and in a wordless flash understands the truth of her being, a truth which is utter simplicity, the original simplicity of all that proceeds from the heart of God.

Jesus, the soul prays, and participates in the power of the Resurrection, the power that breaks the will to war and replaces it with peace, the power that makes the blind to see and the lame to leap and the hungry to be satisfied and the dead to be raised and the abandoned to be embraced into the heart of God.

Jesus, the soul prays, and rejoices that from now on into eternity nothing can separate her from the name that is her life.

I turn on a light and open my prayer book to Morning Prayer. I pick up my guitar, strum the chords of the psalm tone for the opening psalm. The words of these psalms now become the prayer words of Jesus, uttered once again, through me.

THE SOUL IN COMMUNION

I am in the habit of getting to church early and sitting quietly, in preparation for what I soon will savor. I close my eyes and let the shuffling and settling-in sounds gently remind me that I am not alone; I am part of a Christian community.

I am in the habit, on travel days, of sitting quietly, alone, in airports, savoring hidden morsels of divine communion. There, too, I close my eyes, and let the shuffle of feet and the public address messages and the muffled roar of jets and the endless cell phone conversations around me be a gentle reminder in these moments of hidden communion that I am not alone; I am part of the human community.

At home, before dawn on this Sunday morning, I am full of anticipation, not because I have seen the risen Lord but because I still attend the One whose body rests in the tomb but whose soul was spared death. And I imagine the soul of Jesus, through the scourging and the anguish of dying, never wavering from that love which is stronger than death. Attending the One in the tomb, I imagine him praying to his Father in the words of the Psalmist:

> The snares of death encompassed me;
> the pangs of Sheol laid hold on me;
> I suffered distress and anguish.
> Then I called on the name of my Father:
> "O Father, I pray, save my life!" (see Ps 116:3–4)

The psalms were the prayer language of Jesus in communion with his Father. He prayed real prayers, and trusted with real trust, because his trials were real trials that cut like a two-edged sword between his living and his dying. When the sacrifice of his life was complete, from the dark tomb Jesus could pray:

> Return, O my soul, to your rest,
> for the Lord has dealt bountifully with you.
> For you have delivered my soul from death,
> my eyes from tears,
> my feet from stumbling. (vv. 7–8)

In the dark before dawn, as I attend the One who lies in the tomb, I realize that *my soul* is the tomb, the safe place of blessed rest after the long agony of dying; a cool, still resting place where the soul of my Lord rests in the arms of his Father.

Father, the soul prays on the out-breath. *Father!* On the in-breath I feel Jesus' gratitude for his Abba's abiding love. On the out-breath he prays, *Father!*

On the in-breath I am washed in his radical trust. On the out-breath he prays, *Father!*

On the in-breath I am washed in his profound gratitude. On the out-breath he prays, *Father!*

On the in-breath I encounter only the tenderest love between Father and Son. On the out-breath he prays, *Father!*

His life is real. His death is real. His resurrection announces the new reality of the reign of God. His presence animates the soul. His eternal communion with his Abba is real communion, and my being, here and now, is the site of that divine banquet.

I am stunned in this moment when I realize that Jesus, who trusted his Abba, even in his deepest anguish, prays now from the soul-tomb where he rests in adoration: *Father! Father!*

The divine communion of Father, Son, and Holy Spirit continues unendingly and everywhere. It is the movable and ever present feast. In this moment the banquet of their communion is here in this predawn hour, in this soul filled with anticipation.

THE WORD I MEANT TO SAY

I look again at that passage from Romans 8, a passage I have memorized, a passage I call upon often because I do not know how to pray as I ought. I think I do, and then the words multiply as I wrestle with what I am trying to say—as though anything needed to be said, as though I might convince God of my sincerity of heart, my availability, my readiness to participate in God's plan for my life and for this world which I touch.

I wrestle with the words and with just the right crafting of words, when all I really want to say is: *Yes.*

Yes. There, I said it, the word I was trying to find all along. I can say that one word, *Yes,* and know that "God, who searches the heart, knows what is the mind of the Spirit, because the

Spirit intercedes for the saints according to the will of God"
(Rom 8:27).

I enter into the freedom of this one simple, strong word, a
word that restores me to my senses, restores the soul to its proper
center which is the heart and mind of God.

Yes.

I breathe out *Yes*, and breathe in the promise of its fruitful-
ness in my life.

I breathe out *Yes*, and breathe in the sure knowledge of
God's promise of fulfillment in my life.

I breathe out *Yes*, and breathe in the pure, strong, uncom-
plicated faith of the young Mary in the presence of God's mes-
senger Gabriel.

I breathe out *Yes*, and breathe in the Lord's invitation to
abide with him in his agony in the garden as he offers his life to
his Father.

I breathe out *Yes*, and know that it is the truest, fullest,
deepest, most resolute expression of my soul before God. The
word is complete. I can think of nothing more to say, nothing
to add, no conditions or qualifications. Beyond this word I am
speechless. All within me is silent, drawn into the mystery of
God.

Yes, I pray. Dawn breaks. The faintest glimmer of light begins to play on the surface of the river below. Having breathed
forth my *Yes,* my task now is to notice things as they unfold in
the circumstances of this day.

Touching the reign of God in my life . . .

- How does my prayer actually shape my life? How does my prayer shape my relationship with God?

- Reciprocally, how does my life shape my prayer? What specific situations or experiences affect or shape the quality of my prayer?

- In what specific ways does my prayer connect me more intentionally with the circumstances of my life? With the circumstances of my world?

- What one word or phrase draws me into the mystery of God in my life?

- What Scriptures or teachings of my Christian heritage shed light or offer a meaningful way to reflect on the interface of my prayer and my experience?

- What are some key words, images, phrases, feelings, or expressions of prayer that come forward for me at this time?

9

These Bones

FOR MANY years I have known that I would eventually have problems with my bones. I was genetically predisposed. Significant loss of bone density was first discovered back in my mid thirties. So I determined that, starting right then, I would faithfully commit myself to doing all the right things. I would eat the right foods, and get all the right exercise.

As results of subsequent bone density tests got progressively worse, I increased my daily walks, consumed huge amounts of calcium supplements, all in a frantic race to beat the odds. I had a feeling deep in my bones, though, that I was steadily losing ground.

And tonight I sit with the results of the most recent scan. I sit, too, with a broken bone in my left foot, a break which seems simply to have happened.

Bones. I think of the anguish of the prophet Jeremiah, imprisoned in a ministry that has consumed him and from which he cannot run. "If I say, *I will not mention him, or speak any more in his name,*" he ponders, "then within me there is something like a burning fire shut up in my bones" (see Jer 20:9).

"Something like a burning fire," Jeremiah cries out, as though his bones and the marrow in his bones might be aflame with God's relentless and passionate fire.

Fire in the bones, pillar of fire, God's passionate, all-consuming fiery presence. I feel this, too. Not in a prophet's anguish, as Jeremiah felt, but in irreversible surrender to God's total claim on my life, right down to my bones and the marrow of my bones, these bones which are porous, brittle, lacking in strength, but still enflamed by the fire of God's passionate presence.

The letter to the Hebrews speaks of the fiery, penetrating work of the word of God within the human soul, the word of God which is "living and active, sharper than any two-edged sword, piercing until it divides soul from spirit, joints from marrow," able to judge the intentions of the heart (Heb 4:12). I too encounter God's searing, penetrating presence, which no part of my being can escape, God's fiery presence rolling through me like ball lightning, setting my inner being on fire.

I sit in the still dark night with God's fire in my bones, these porous, brittle bones. I imagine small bright flames lapping out through the honeycomb holes. I imagine a warm glow, as one would find at the hearth on a wintry night. Like the burning bush before Moses, this fire burns; it engulfs me, yet I am not consumed. I know, deep in my bones, that I am irreversibly God's yet I live; as St. Paul writes, "it is no longer I who live, but it is Christ who lives in me" (Gal 2:20). I am consumed in the fire of God's truth and love, yet miraculously not destroyed.

In fact, a new unexpected strength stirs deep in the marrow of my bones, a new strength which is a quiet and sure knowing of divine presence which I cannot describe. I feel certain that in the deep dark silence of my being, these bones are being rekindled, reknit, renewed in ways which will become clear in some future bone scan.

I drink from the bowl of Fire, the cup of salvation, the chalice of the Lord's fiery and precious blood. The wordless knowledge of this Fire penetrates deep into my bones and the marrow of my bones.

Could it be that my soul resides in my bones and in the marrow of my bones? I have always imagined my soul residing elsewhere. If my soul resides in my bones and in the marrow of my bones, does it mean that my soul is porous and brittle, too? Or does it mean that the soul's dwelling in these honeycombed bones is capable of renewing and strengthening them?

I am not speaking metaphorically here, but of an actual experience, a new reality, these bones becoming a new creation in Christ.

Touching the reign of God in my life . . .

- What physical, mental, or emotional condition offers me an unexpected entry into the mystery of God at work in my life? What is that experience for me?

- When I sit quietly with this physical, mental, or emotional condition, what conversation does it seem to have with God? What gets said in that dialogue? What might God be revealing to me uniquely in this condition?

- Does this condition reflect the challenge or the grace of some other aspect of my life? What aspect of my life, and how so?

- What Scriptures or teachings of my Christian heritage shed light or offer a meaningful way to reflect on this condition?

- What are some key words, images, phrases, feelings, or expressions of prayer that come forward for me at this time?

10

Triumph of Extreme Humility

IN THE hour before the first trace of dawn, a half harvest moon hangs in the western sky. Even through the thick double screens on my apartment windows I see stars twinkling in a cloudless sky, promise of a brilliant dawn.

The street below is quiet now. The downtown bars closed two hours ago, and all the revelrous young Saturday night patrons, surely now asleep, will not awaken for a very long time.

I have prepared my prayer table for today's feast, the Triumph of the Cross, September 14th. The only light in the room comes from a votive candle, a small flame dancing in a red glass holder on the prayer table. This small flickering flame casts a suggestion of light onto the items I have brought to the day's prayer: a thin rugged piece of petrified tree branch affixed by twine to a tall wooden stand, reaching its gnarled form thirty inches upward from the base, and beside it, a diminutive, dark-toned icon.

The gnarled, petrified tree branch I have had for maybe thirty years, a cast-off of nature from a hillside in western Oregon, gift of a Trappist monk who handed it to me, saying nothing, knowing that I would see what he could see in this branch: its two extended arms, the darkened smudge of face, and hollowed core, altogether suggesting the agonized spirit of the crucified Christ.

The small sacred icon on the prayer table is new. When I first saw it I was startled, at once recoiling yet irresistibly drawn by its dark and terrible beauty. I had never seen such a depiction of the crucified Lord, revealing to me starkly what I must become, since I am his. The icon's title: Christ, Extreme Humility.

Against the icon's black background of a darkened cosmos that has lost its Light I see the torso, arms, and head of the crucified Christ, eyes closed in the sleep of death. The face no longer expresses agony or spiritual anguish but rather the self-forgetfulness of a man exhausted, completely spent, stripped of the dignity of life, who has surrendered, at last, to the consolation of the great final sleep.

His arms are the arms of one completely emaciated, mere bone sheathed in fragile flesh. Collarbone and ribs nearly pierce through his tissue-thin skin. A gash in his side is underlined by a last dried trickle of blood. The circle of light behind his sacred head is the color of a low harvest moon.

The sacred body of this disfigured One, once heralded by angels and archangels, now descends alone into the small blood-red box of a tomb. Behind him is the wood figure of the cross, two nails to his right and to his left, hammered into the cross beam. Above his head float two objects that look like blood silver coins, with the inscriptions *IC* and *XC,* meaning: Jesus Christ.

And upright beside him in the blood-red box are elements of his torture and humiliation: an elongated spear on the left and on the right a thin reed tipped with the wine-soaked sponge.

There is in the body of this crucified Christ no loveliness of a favored Son, no royal beauty, no kingly strength. Yet against the dark background a holy serenity glows from the face, the flesh. The sleep of death comes as a mercy for this One who disposed himself completely to his Father's divine plan and emptied himself of all claim to favor. "You who are great must become the least," we remember him saying, "if you would enter into the reign of God." He taught us, and now he has shown us, the price of love strong enough to rebind the human heart to the heart of God. He leads the way for all who would dare to follow him on the path of obedience and self-surrender, for he also said, "I am the way."

This image before me reveals what I would rather not see: Extreme humility, the ravaged remains of extreme humiliation.

I play at practicing humility, I secretly admit, and that is no humility at all. In those rare moments when I set aside my rightful claim and defer to others, I am quietly pleased with myself for this subtle and noble gesture. But I miss the point entirely. Being pleased, even quietly pleased, with my small acts of humility is an affront to the One who is Extreme Humility. My hollow virtue is my defeat.

I do not know humility. I have not tasted humility, not really. In situations where I could have humbled myself I have resisted; I have fired back flaming arrows of righteous indignation. Without hesitation I have spoken up to justify my words, my actions, my position, in moral self-defense, self-sure and fighting to the end. Why should I buckle before an oppressor?

But in the eyes of God everything looks different. In the eyes of God I have nothing to boast about and nothing, really, to defend. "O Lord, I am your servant; . . . you have loosed my bonds," the Psalmist sings (Ps 116:16). And St. Paul writes that Christ Jesus, though he was God, set aside his divine glory and entered into human flesh and circumstance, enduring humiliation and death, "even death on a cross" (see Phil 2:6–8).

As I look upon this image of Christ, Extreme Humility, I see not the radiant physical presence of a favored Son, but the last shreds of powerlessness, the unexplainable wastefulness of a foolishly loving God, here in the guise of a crucified common criminal. He who did not know sin became sin for our sake,

St. Paul writes, so that in him we might become the righteousness of God (see 2 Cor 5:21). This is the extreme foolishness of
the soul's true Lover. Crucified between two thieves, Jesus in all
humility is the Good Thief, stealing from me my debt of sin,
a debt too great for me to bear. And more, he steals from me
my identity before God—my self-imposed identity of sinner,
betrayer, imposter, pretender to greatness. And he, true Lover,
gives me a new identity: his own.

This feast of the Triumph of the Cross could be called the
feast of the Triumph of Extreme Humility, an odd combination
of terms. I think of triumph as the celebration of victory, celebration of a final, complete, definitive win over an opponent.
Triumph and victory are terms of battle, where evil is overcome
and good wins, endures. These are terms of power, and so they
are dangerous terms. The cross can be used, and tragically has
been used, as a bullying force to expand Christendom. But
Extreme Humility is incapable of bullying. It is a force of divine
love that does not coerce but evokes and invites and proposes an
unimagined entry into God's unimaginable life.

Before this image of Christ I am reduced to silence. Sin
is not a trifle; it is a partnership with death. He who did not
know sin became sin for my sake, for the sake of each and every
one, for the sake of us all. Love is foolish. Divine love knows no
limits. As I look upon this One who, without hesitation, became
Extreme Humility for my sake, I see costly love poured out,
utterly spent. I look at the dark, obstinate, prideful elements of
my life and wonder sometimes if God's costly love was poured
out in vain.

Yet Extreme Humility will not be God's final word, for
God "highly exalted him and gave him the name that is above
every name" (Phil 2:9). To speak the lovely, humble, and trium-
phant name of Jesus is to proclaim the glory of God the Father,
in the power and grace of the Holy Spirit.

On this Sunday morning I sit quietly, reflecting on this feast of the Triumph of the Cross, settling my soul in quiet anticipation of the divine-human communion soon to take place. As dawn yields to the full light of day I find myself sinking deep into a word which whispers itself new with each breath, a word prayed with great and tender passion, growing in magnitude like an ocean swell. I awaken once more to this lovely word, "Father," prayed with a reverence that runs like a river of grace through my body, and I awaken to the One who is praying the word through me, Jesus himself, Extreme Humility.

This, too, I discover, is extreme humility: That Jesus should be pleased to speak adoringly to his Father through one as inconstant as me.

Touching the reign of God in my life . . .

- What does Jesus' suffering and death reveal to me about the reign of God?

- What circumstances of powerlessness or injustice in my own experience come to mind?

- Can I say that my experience was in some way a participation in Jesus' experience of humility, humiliation, and surrender at the hands of evil? If I endured this test poorly, how might I now make it right?

- What Scriptures or teachings of my Christian heritage shed light or offer a meaningful way to reflect on these circumstances in my life?

- What are some key words, images, phrases, feelings, or expressions of prayer that come forward for me at this time?

11

True Love

A Reflection on the Essence of Christian Life

"ABOVE ALL, maintain constant love for one another," I read in the first letter of St. Peter, "for love covers a multitude of sins" (1 Pet 4:8).

Constant love? I feel exhausted at the mere *thought* of maintaining constant love for the people in my life. The threshold is too high, I protest, impossible to reach. The phrase stuns me, stings me; it comes as a spiritual challenge which I instinctively know I will never meet, and so it convicts me of my smallness of heart. "Above all," Peter begins, meaning: Treat this as the highest priority. "Above all" comes as a warning: *Pay attention! I am telling you something important!*

What does this mean, to "maintain constant love for one another"? Constant love does not happen by chance; it is an intentional love, a love that not merely accepts but searches out the unloved and unlovely places in the other, because none of us is constantly lovely or lovable—not by human standards. And which "other" am I to love? The Scripture passage suggests "each" other, particularly and individually, and that would include everyone who is not me.

LOVE AS FOUNDATION

That a particular, individual love "for one another" exists at all reveals the essence of the Christian community, because this particular, individual love is the very foundation of Christian life and practice. These words from the first letter of St. Peter speak the same truth preached by St. Paul: True love, real love, enduring and worthy love, love that redeems and restores, originates not with me but with the One who has claimed me as his dwelling place. "It is no longer I who live, but it is Christ who lives in me," Paul tells the Christian community (Gal 2:20). My life, and therefore my loves, are not my own.

"Let your love for one another be of a whole different quality," Peter might write, "than the love of those who have not yet entered into Christ." The first letter of St. John says as much, too: "Beloved, let us love one another, because love is from God; everyone who loves is born of God and knows God" (1 John 4:7); and again, "Beloved, since God loved us so much, we also ought to love one another. No one has ever seen God; if we love one another, God lives in us, and his love is perfected in us" (vv. 11–12).

Faithfully living this Christian life of love seems an impossible task. In fact, it often can feel like an onerous chore, designed to induce a sense of perpetual guilt. So the challenge, it seems, is not to love harder, but to intentionally let the love of Christ—not my love, but his love—burn more intensely, flow more freely, in me and through me. And here is the challenge: I must agree to this power of Christ's love having its healing, reconciling, disarming effect in me and through me. I must submit to it, give my unqualified Yes to it. I must let the power of Christ's love rule my heart, tame it, control it, harness it for God's purposes. My task, it seems, is to make space for this enormous love to have its way in me. I must choose to cooperate with Christ—work together with Christ, source of this intense love—so that his love can effectively touch and ignite the lives of others.

WHOSE SIN DOES LOVE COVER?

Love each other constantly, Peter writes, "for love covers a multitude of sins." It seems to me that when one is covered with love, the Lord's own cloak of mercy covers all that is ugly and shameful, covers all that betrays the image of God's beauty.

But what is Peter suggesting here? Is it the multitude of sins of the person I love that becomes covered by love? Or is it *my* multitude of sins that becomes covered when I love another constantly? Possibly both. Yes, certainly both. When I love others, something dynamic is set in motion. They indeed are changed by love, even if only by degrees, and so am I.

Yet most especially, I believe, it is the other's multitude of sins that is covered in my loving the other constantly, because my love—if I can call it mine—embodies and sets in motion Christ's redemptive love, covering sin with his cloak of mercy, and restoring that one to right relationship with himself, with his Father, and with the human community.

So my participation in Christ's redemptive work frees me to love not only those who love me, or those to whom I feel drawn, but I become free to love those who are most in need of Christ's mercy and redemption. If I am honest about this redemptive work of love, then I will be led by the Holy Spirit—the power of Christ's love within me—to love constantly those whose sin in fact may repulse me. If I truly accept the challenge of love, then I will be compelled to love even those who seem obnoxious or blatantly offensive, or who have wounded me deeply.

St. Peter insists: Let your love for one another be deep, intense, genuine, restorative. He is not speaking of generally loving the multitudes, but loving constantly, deeply, and intentionally those particular ones within the circles of relationship and circumstance in our lives who, like us, bear the burden of a multitude of sins. Christ in his mercy longs to heal us, particularly, individually, and all of us together, healing and loving each of us as though there were only one of us.

Touching the reign of God in my life . . .

- In what specific, tangible ways do I experience the reign of God in others' constant love for me? How has that love restored me, renewed me, or allowed me simply to be myself?

- What have I experienced when I intentionally practiced a "continual love" for someone whose behavior or attitude has angered or repulsed me?

- If I have loved poorly, how might I make amends and start over? What specific actions would "starting over" require of me?

- What Scriptures or teachings of my Christian heritage shed light or offer a meaningful way to reflect on these circumstances?

- What are some key words, images, phrases, feelings, or expressions of prayer that come forward for me at this time?

12

Let My Prayer Arise

Meditations on Morning, Evening, and Night Prayer

I

"O LORD, OPEN MY LIPS"

Morning Prayer

EARLY MORNING, for me, is a privileged time, a uniquely spiritual time. Not that it is more sacred than other times of day, for all time, as God's gift, is sacred.

But that first pulse of early morning—that first awareness of how I feel when I awaken—offers me an immediate, unedited reading on where I stand with my life, and therefore where I stand with God.

In that first moment of awakening, I may feel energized by the prospect of work that engages my best talents; I may feel sullen with unforgiven hurtful words of the day before. I may feel a knot in the pit of my stomach, knowing that within hours I will undergo a challenge I would rather not face.

In that first moment of awakening, I may feel loved, or abandoned; hopeful, or weary; full of purpose, or lost. I may feel surprised by the beauty of dawn, or dampened by yet one more day of overcast.

I find comfort and encouragement in knowing that the Church, in daily liturgical prayer, gives me a way to lift up and dedicate my being before God in the new day. Morning after morning the praying Church cries out as one body, in one voice, "O Lord, open my lips, and my mouth will declare your praise" (Ps 51:15).

I first heard this opening antiphon of Morning Prayer chanted gently in the dark, cool morning stillness by Trappist monks when I was a child. Ever since then, my heart has been stirred by these words filled with holy possibility in the new day. Invoking the Lord, I acknowledge that I am the Lord's; my being, my life, is the Lord's. My first words of prayer remind me that I am not the center, not the moving force, of my life.

Morning by morning I am moved by the grace of a fresh start, the gift of God's loving-kindness. In every season of the Church's year, in every season of my life, this one simple phrase causes my soul to rise in the wonder of God's presence and movement in my life, now, in this new day. This phrase awakens within me the mystery of Incarnation, God enfleshed here and now.

What is the context of this brief yet stirring phrase: "O Lord, open my lips, and my mouth will declare your praise"? What does it reveal of the gift of Jesus' Incarnation and my immersion in the rhythm of his life, death, and resurrection?

Psalm 51: From Sinfulness to Celebration of God's Mercy

How fitting that the first words of the Church at prayer each morning come from a psalm that confesses human sinfulness and prays for the grace of conversion of heart. Psalm 51 is attributed to King David, after Nathan approaches him about David's sinful deed toward Bathsheba and his cover-up instruction to have her husband Uriah killed in battle.

"Why have you despised the word of the Lord, to do what is evil in his sight?" Nathan stingingly asks (2 Sam 12:9a). In reply David confesses, simply, "I have sinned against the Lord" (v. 13a). No excuses are offered, no attempts made at self-justification. And Nathan answers David: "Now the Lord has put away your sin; you shall not die" (v. 13b).

In an opening verse of Psalm 51 the Psalmist prays, "Wash me thoroughly from my iniquity and cleanse me from my sin." No effort is made to downplay the guilt for sinful deeds, nor to point a finger of blame elsewhere:

> For I know my transgressions,
> and my sin is ever before me.
> Against you, you only, have I sinned,
> and done what is evil in your sight. (Ps 51:3–4)

Following a prayer for sincerity of heart and for God's gift of wisdom, the Psalmist pleads, "Purge me, . . . wash me. . . . Let me hear joy and gladness" (vv. 7–8). I hear in these words a plea for deep cleansing of heart and spirit, anticipatory longing for baptismal cleansing, letting the old self die and hoping for rebirth in God's presence. The human spirit stirs at the mere thought of new life before God and the Psalmist issues a plea:

> Create in me a clean heart, O God,
> and put a new and right spirit within me.
> Do not cast me away from your presence,
> and do not take your holy spirit from me.
> (vv. 10–11)

Renewed in God's mercy and favor, the Psalmist vows to live to God's glory and promises to "teach transgressors your ways, and sinners will return to you" (v. 13). The Psalmist indeed heralds the promise of baptismal immersion into Christ's paschal mystery: Death of sinful self and rising to new life in God. Forgiven of sin and the guilt of sin, and renewed in God's spirit, now the Psalmist prays:

> O Lord, open my lips,
> and my mouth will declare your praise. (v. 15)

The Hebrew understanding of the psalms was so deep and so thorough that to pray one line of a psalm was to evoke the entire psalm. And so, as I recite that opening antiphon of Morning Prayer, that one lovely line from Psalm 51, I pray not only for the gift of cleansed lips to proclaim God's praises, but for the gift of God's cleansing mercy toward my sinfulness, both hidden and revealed, in every aspect of my life.

I pray for the continued cleansing work of baptism and for the strength and vigor of renewal in God's Spirit and in the body of Christ. Each morning I join my solitary voice to the voice of the entire praying Church—not just the Church worldwide in this particular morning hour, but the Church past and future, too. In praying this opening antiphon, I acknowledge that from human brokenness and longing for wholeness God's praises pour forth and rise up.

A Daily Immersion in Christ's Paschal Mystery

I spend a fair amount of my work day rummaging around the creative workshop of my imagination, where Scripture and prayer and reflection on the circumstances of a life lived in Christ come together in unexpected ways. I am content to let my imagination be a sandbox for the Holy Spirit. My work flows forth from this fluid environment, where all kinds of things come together—words I read, bits of conversation, a phrase from a homily, a passage from Scripture, an image from a poem, something in the news, kind deeds of strangers, the stuff of daily experience. I am inspired by the gifts of creation, the turn of seasons, a fresh encounter with symbol or metaphor, a heartfelt moment of friendship. These experiences feed my imagination and shape my prayer, because they connect me, flesh and spirit, to my creating, redeeming God. In my daily living the wonder of Incarnation continues to unfold.

So "opening my lips" (or my writer's pen), as in the phrase, "O Lord, open my lips," is not a first act but a second act—a fruit, really, of the conscious and prayerful and creative act of living in that place where experience, imagination, and understanding intersect, that place of dynamic mystery where the Holy Spirit dwells.

From the sandbox of imagination I take what I have gathered "into the studio" for some analytical and creative work—into the studio of mind and heart. This creative process is not unique to people who write or speak for their livelihood. It is the gift given, to one degree or another, in one aspect of life or another, to every human being who is made in the image and likeness of God (see Gen 1:26–27). Through our faithful living of often quite ordinary yet graced lives, and reflection upon our experience, the Word continues to become flesh and make its dwelling among us (see John 1:14a).

One morning, as I brought my life before God at the opening of Morning Prayer, I traced the sign of the Cross on my lips and prayed the opening antiphon.

"O Lord, open my lips," I uttered. But I stopped.

This gesture is not big enough, I thought; *this phrase does not capture what I mean.*

"What is it," I asked myself, "that I am trying to communicate with these words, and to express with my life?"

So I began the opening antiphon again, but this time with the threefold blessing of forehead, lips, and heart, tracing on each the sign of the Cross as I prayed:

> Lord, open my mind and my imagination ✠
> my lips ✠
> and my heart ✠
> and my *life* this day will proclaim your praise.

Ah! That's it! This prayer now feels big enough. Like Mary in her hymn of praise, my entire being rises up daily to proclaim the greatness of the Lord (see Luke 1:46).

What an offering of self-before-God this prayer becomes, what a plea for sanctification of all I will do throughout the day. When I dedicate "all my heart and all my soul and all my mind and all my strength" (see Matt 22:37; Deut 6:5) to proclaim God's praise, are not these core aspects of my being—heart, imagination, mind, and strength—surely blessed?

Of course they are. Throughout the day I become aware of how God showers me with the grace to stay alert, ready to receive the gifts of heart and soul and mind and strength, to create and share with others whatever will proclaim God's praise. These graces had been given to me all along. What really changes with this opening antiphon is my awareness of God's graces and my eagerness and joy to receive them. When I ask for God's blessing on the circumstances of my life, God is compelled by love to say *Yes!* The mystery of Incarnation continues to unfold.

In baptism I am incorporated into the body of Christ, and I spend a lifetime living out this mystery, leaning in total trust into God's perfect plan for my fullness of life in God's presence.

No matter how broken we may feel by sin or disappointment, no matter how weary from the journey—up the rough side of the mountain or across the blazing desert—no aspect of human life falls outside of God's care. The Church invites us, fresh each day, to set aside the isolating illusion of self-sufficiency, to pray for forgiveness, and to ask for the grace to proclaim God's praise with our whole being, in space and time, in word and deed, in the day ahead.

II

"LIKE THE EVENING SACRIFICE"

Evening Prayer

Perhaps at no moment in the day is the sanctification of human experience through prayer more meaningful and gracious than in the evening. Evening Prayer invites me to honor the rhythm of rest after labor, and to release the work of my hands and the concerns of heart and mind as I make of them an offering to God.

"All is yours, Lord," the heart says at the evening hour, as Evening Prayer opens with the antiphon:

> Let my prayer be counted as incense before you,
> and the lifting up of my hands as an evening
> sacrifice. (Ps 141:2)

Let My Prayer Be Incense, A Fragrant Offering to God

In the Hebrew Scriptures we find the sacred practice of tithing, as the Israelites offered the choicest first fruits of their labor to God in honor and thanksgiving. The offerings—the first produce of the soil and best firstlings of the flock—are burnt, and their smoke rises, becoming a prayer-offering to God. The offering is complete and irretrievable; nothing remains in the ashes which one might take back for personal benefit.

Such complete offering—now, as then—celebrates God, source of abundant generosity. In the offering, I give freely back to God what God has freely given to me. My prayer of evening offering is a bold act of surrender and trust, my daily participation in Christ Jesus' pouring out of self before his Father.

In the book of Exodus, Moses receives instruction from God on how to build the altar at which "Aaron shall offer fragrant incense . . . every morning . . . and when Aaron sets up the lamps in the evening" (Exod 30:7–8).

Morning after morning, God instructs us, and again each evening, we are to gather for ritual prayer in praise and thanksgiving to God.

In today's busy world, it is seldom easy to find time for the ritual of daily prayer. In a culture that spins around compulsive busyness, endless chatter, and information overload, quieting down body, mind, and spirit for daily prayer would seem to consume precious time and yield nothing of real value. Such gathering and pausing before God does not appear "productive." In fact, prayer would seem to interrupt our productivity.

For many of us, much of the time, we believe that we cannot afford to slow down and carve out a time of rest before supper or at twilight, to make of ourselves and our day, in Christ, a pleasing offering to God. We prefer to not lose our grip on time by interrupting it with something as low priority as prayer.

Yet, imagine the gentle rhythm of Evening Prayer, a graceful interruption in a runaway day, a brief prayerful interlude with no radio, no TV, no phone conversations in traffic, no family members tugging at us, no racing toward the next round of activities. Imagine a time, even if brief, of evening psalms, prayers of praise and thanksgiving, time set aside, a momentary grace-filled resting in God. This tithed and holy time casts all other concerns in a new and holy light.

For a few restful minutes we can release who-we-are and what-we-do as an offering to God, allowing the risen Christ to transform our sometimes disjointed and imperfect efforts of the day into his perfect work of salvation, rising like fragrant incense before God.

That is the point of Evening Prayer. Nothing more. Just a freewill offering of self, of things accomplished, things unfinished, things mishandled or failed; an offering of the labors and hopes and pain of the world, the lifting up of all of creation back to a generous and tender-hearted, merciful, and all-worthy God. Such surrender in offering to God comes as blessed relief.

Evening Prayer reminds me that there is one God, all-worthy, all-powerful, who invites me to lay my burdens down, knowing that with the morning comes fresh praise and renewed strength of body, mind, and spirit.

My Hands Uplifted in Evening Sacrifice

From the smoke of first fruits ascending as free offering, to the ritual use of temple incense at break of day and at its close, to supplication embodied in hands lifted to God, prayer ultimately involves the whole self. "Every day I call on you, O Lord," the Psalmist sings; "I spread out my hands to you" (Ps 88:9).

Jesus, too, stretched out his hands to God, and the embodied prayer of torn flesh and anguished spirit became the ultimate and total offering of self to God. After his resurrection Jesus told Peter that he, Peter, also would stretch out his hands and would be led where he would rather not go, to make of his life a pleasing offering to God (see John 21:18). As faithful followers of Christ Jesus, we are sobered by these words. The lifting of hands in evening sacrifice becomes a symbolic gesture that releases a reality and sets it in motion: Our passage, alone and together, in total trust, into the mystery of death and resurrection in Christ is unconditional, without reservation.

Must I journey that far into death of self, as Evening Prayer suggests? Must my emptying of self be total, with nothing held back in reserve? In the moment of my earthly dying I know that I will undergo a total death of physical self and come, by grace, to fullness of life in God. The work of Jesus' paschal mystery will be accomplished in me, perfectly, now or later. I am his and more than his: I am part of the very body of the incarnate and risen Christ.

The symbol of fragrant smoke rising, in the opening antiphon of Evening Prayer, speaks eloquently: My offering is personal, total, and irreversible. Nothing retrievable remains in the ash of incense, in the ash of self-offering. No part of my self can be held back from God in the evening offering: Not the personal agenda nor the unforgiving grudge nor the need to be front, center and best; not the heartfelt plea nor the well-intentioned longing for my fulfillment or someone else's good. All of it becomes offering to God, released from my uplifted hands into the open hands of God.

My uplifted hands and the physical gesture of lifting up my life this day, both become prayer. My trusting spirit and the conscious act of letting go, these too become my prayer. Self-becoming-prayer in this opening antiphon of Evening Prayer evokes the image of the small child, all trusting, stretching arms upward to the next friendly adult, in a gesture that says, "Hold me, lift me up," a gesture of dependence and trust. The gesture may further mean "Relieve me of this dirty diaper," or it may mean "Put me to bed; I need to rest now," or "Feed me," or "Cover me with hugs and kisses." But always, the gesture is a surrender in trust that "someone who is greater than me will understand me and care for my needs."

Evening Prayer invites me to do the same, to surrender to God and trust that this utterly gracious Other, all-worthy of my trust and the offering of my life, will care for my needs and, in the risen Christ, make me whole.

III

"DO NOT HIDE YOUR FACE FROM ME"

Night Prayer

Sometimes late at night when I am too tired to pray, I ask the Holy Spirit to pray in me. I have prayed Night Prayer, or Compline, the prayer marking the completion of day, for most of my adult life. And now I often pray much of Night Prayer from memory, by heart, with my eyes closed.

Once in a while my thoughts drift somewhere deep in the prayer. In moments like this I trust that the Holy Spirit is at work, interceding for me with deep inexpressible groanings that cannot be formed into words (see Rom 8:26).

One night as I began praying Night Prayer, I closed my eyes and prayed, *Do not hide your face from me; in you I put my trust.* I do not recall whether I stayed awake to pray the psalm, but I know that the antiphon took me somewhere I had not expected.

Once I prayed the antiphon and felt it settle in, I became confused, disoriented within my imagination. At first I thought I had misunderstood the words of the antiphon, but was this a misunderstanding or a graced insight?

Do Not Hide Your Face from Me

The Holy Spirit, I know with certainty, really does pray in me—not always in my voice but sometimes in God's voice. And God was speaking to me, clearly, gently, and personally this night.

"Do not hide your face from me!" I heard God plead. That clear, quiet voice called me to attention, and I felt as though the eyes of God were riveted on me, a laser look of love that pleaded for my undivided heart.

I felt the quiet authority of this voice; I sensed the compelling command. As a parent might say to a child, *"Look at me when I speak to you!"* I knew I could not turn away. I sensed too the calm and certain authority of the Teacher. "Do *not* hide your eyes, your heart, your faith from me," I imagined the Lord saying. Matthew tells us of Jesus' teaching to the multitudes on the mountainside (see Matt 5–7). "Do *not* hide your face from me," he might well have pleaded, "I share with you words from the very heart of God."

Yet God's plea to me this night carried something more. It was a prayerful supplication, whispered pleadingly to the beloved: *"Do not hide your face from me. Though others may turn away, please, do not turn away from me."*

I recalled Jesus' hauntingly vulnerable words to the Twelve when others were leaving his company, unable to take his teaching on the Bread of Life: "Do you also want to leave me?" he asks (see John 6:67).

My heart replies with the words of Peter: "Lord, to whom can I go? You have the words of eternal life" (v. 68). The mere thought of leaving this One who calls me "beloved" wounds and confuses me, and the confession spills forth: "You are my way, my truth, my life" (see John 14:6).

As my mind and heart drift between prayer and sleep, I am stunned by what I discover: *Love makes God vulnerable.*

God, untiring lover of human hearts, waits as I choose a hundred times a day between honoring and embracing this relationship of enduring covenant love, or choosing "other gods" who only increase my sorrows (see Ps 16:4a).

God waits on me. This is the amazing and humbling thing. God waits on my choices to love or to not love. The heart of God incarnate feels pain, grieves at my misguided passions and empty choices. How easily I turn away, lose myself in distractions. I am capable of engaging in death-dealing of every sort. Yet God waits on me, waits on my choices to love or to not love.

"Do not hide your face from me," the voice of All Love echoes down through the ages. We have heard God's voice through the voice of the prophets calling us to our senses. Daily we hear God's voice through the voice of the broken ones, the despised, the disenfranchised, the dispossessed, all of them fragile and calling us to act on behalf of compassion, justice, and mercy. The incarnate and risen Christ pleads, *"Do not hide your face from me!"*

God indeed is vulnerable in love. We can turn to oh so many other "authorities," other so-called teachers, and they all have a program to sell us. We can seek what pleases our ears and soothes our troubled conscience; we can gorge ourselves on a cheaper love, we who have no end of lifestyle options smartly packaged for our delight.

But the outcome can never be the same. The fruit of our cheaper loves, in the end, is loathsome, a rotting fruit that leaves us restless with hunger. *"Do not hide your face from me,"* God pleads, for we do have other options; daily we make our choices.

In You I Put My Trust

What might these words mean, if God were pleading, *"Do not hide your face from me,"* adding, astonishingly and humbly, *"in you I put my trust"*? That God should put trust in me? That God should become, in this relationship of trust and love, like a child, a beloved, like one who waits and hopes?

"In you I put my trust." From the very beginning God has trusted the likes of you and me. From the beginning God entrusted all of creation to our care. Have we honored that trust? God entrusted the Beloved Son to us. Did we honor that supreme gift of Love-among-us then? And do we honor that divine gift now? Why, then, should God continue to say to the likes of you and me, *"In you I put my trust"*?

When the One who is the source and fullness of my being says to me, "In you I put my trust," I am irresistibly claimed by Love in a powerful, redeeming, life-giving way. I am compelled to leave my self-serving ways and enter honestly, humbly, into this relationship which acknowledges my being worthy of divine trust. I stand, washed by the blood of the Lamb, in relationship with this One who breathes forth my being, calls me by my name, and sustains my life by a mighty love.

"In you I put my trust," God says. I am entrusted with the awesome and holy work of pouring out fully all that I am and rising to new life in the person of the Beloved Son.

"Let me lean on you," God might say. "Let me count on you. Let me count on your heart, your imagination, your in- tentions and choices. Let me count on your presence and your constancy in being in my love and standing in my place before others."

Now Incarnation takes on a fresh and deeper meaning within my flesh. I am the body of Christ; and if not me, then who? "My flesh . . . true food, and my blood . . . true drink," my life poured out, small portions at a time, that others might live. I am the body of Christ, and one day I shall be called by that name, when my life and all of creation become, at last, the one perfect and pleasing offering in Christ Jesus to God the Father.

"In you I put my trust," God says, and I know that I now have a part in the work of redemption, doing that part for which I have been anointed. *"In you I put my trust . . . to carry my compassion and to speak my truth and to heal with my mercy and to nurture and restore from my great abundance."*

Amen. Night Prayer is complete. I sleep, at peace in God.

Touching the reign of God in my life . . .

- What specific words or phrases in these reflections on Morning, Evening, and Night Prayer help me to touch the reign of God revealed in my own life?

- If God places trust in me, in my faithfulness in this unparalleled relationship of love, how specifically do I honor that trust? In what specific ways might I more intentionally honor and act on God's trust in me?

- What daily prayer practices currently help me to draw near to, touch, and enter into the reign of God? What are some instances where my prayer has led me to encounter the reign of God in my life?

- What Scriptures or teachings of my Christian heritage shed light or offer a meaningful way to reflect on the regular and meaningful prayer practices in my life?

- What are some key words, images, phrases, feelings, or expressions of prayer that come forward for me at this time?

13

Reconciled in Christ

WORLD NEWS again is not good. Well, today what this means is that a terrorist plot was discovered to use liquid explosives on flights coming into the United States. This captures our attention because it means that an actual plan to harm unsuspecting U.S. citizens has been uncovered.

It is difficult for me to wrap my imagination around the reality of a war that rages daily on someone else's soil. Our troops are "there," in a place where "those people" don't look like "us." In fact, anyone here who looks like "them" is apt to be treated with suspicion. All of this is crazy making.

In one way it's crazy making because we now have a world full of people who live in the grip of fear—the paralyzing source of unfreedom and the catalyst for equally irrational and somehow perfectly justified response.

But at a deeper level the condition of the world is crazy making because in our desperation we forget that the human agony we experience or witness is the agony of Christ, that he bears this current human agony, as he has carried all human agonies, in his flesh, which is our human flesh. We thresh around feverish and frustrated in the world's agony because we have forgotten the hope and promise of redemption, not only for ourselves but for all of humankind. We live as if the Jesus of history and the Christ of faith left no footprints.

St. Paul calls us back to our senses:

> But now in Christ Jesus you who once were far off
> have been brought near by the blood of Christ.
> For he is our peace; in his flesh he has made both
> groups into one and has broken down the divid-
> ing wall, that is, the hostility between us. He has
> abolished the law with its commandments and or-
> dinances, that he might create in himself one new
> humanity in place of the two, thus making peace,
> and might reconcile both groups to God in one
> body through the cross, thus putting to death that
> hostility through it. (Eph 2:13–16)

You who once were far off. I think about this phrase which
is deeper, perhaps, than it appears. "Once," it says, suggesting
that our situation now is different, that where we once were is
not where we are now. Yet our reality, I think, the reality we see
today on our TV screens and hear in the news, suggests that we
still are far off, very far off. Hopelessly far off, one is tempted
to say.

"Far off," St. Paul writes. "Far away," I think at first, "far
distant" as in a physical, geographical wandering.

"Far off the mark" is the phrase that catches me, the phrase
I would rather not look at, rather not touch. Far off the mark,
as in sinful, erring grievously, missing the mark sometimes by
existential inches, sometimes missing the mark completely.

"You have been brought near," St. Paul writes. Brought near.
Not "together," or "enmeshed," or "made one," but "brought
near." Disarmed enough to approach the possibility of trust and
the experience of a new reality in Christ, the new, disarmed and
disarming reality of grace which is the reign of God.

And this is no temporary or half-measure nearness. It is
not a truce enforced by so-called "peacekeepers." The nearness

which St. Paul describes is not tentative but decisive and radically transforming, because we have been brought near "by the blood of Christ," he writes, "for he is our peace."

In his flesh and blood, in his living and dying and rising, Christ Jesus is our peace; in his invitation to healing and wholeness and reconciliation, Christ Jesus is our peace. "Through his flesh," St. Paul writes, through the insertion of his life and his Spirit into our torn reality, Christ Jesus is our peace. He tears our tornness in two; he rends our rent histories and all the shards of abandoned relationships and betrayed trust in two. He rends in two our incapacity to imagine life whole and animated by God's life-giving Spirit.

All this rending of what is lifeless and untrue to our humanity is so that "he might create in himself one new person in place of the two, thus establishing peace."

In this most simple yet challenging phrase, we are offered the recipe for peace. Peace is not *our* accomplishment, not *our* doing, but in the Spirit of the risen Christ peace is *done unto* us, assuming we submit our proud and hollow posturing to God's restorative work. The blood of Christ Jesus is more powerful than all the empty power the world can scheme and plot and hatch. The blood of Christ Jesus sears the festering boils of falsehood off the soul of humankind—already, yes, but not yet completely. Divine humility's triumph over human arrogance endures even while evil carves its tortuous path of greed, terror, war, and death.

By his cross and in his flesh, Christ Jesus reconciles us in God, holds us together in the one eternal unitive embrace: Already, but not yet completely. We still twist in anguish and fear.

How do governments and leaders of nations bring about peace? How do we get agents of fear and destruction to come to their senses, put away their bombs, walk away from their

isolative cells and dark networks, and come into the human circle, the circle of humanity in which true peace longs to reside?

I cannot make peace happen. I wish I could. The best I
can do, I believe, is to submit my own life, my own attitudes
and resistances and fears, to the deep work of peace which the
risen Lord bestowed as a first fruit of his resurrection. His peace
is the new reality, the new order which is powerful enough to
refashion the human community, riddled with dysfunction, into
a human community that eventually will "be one, as we are one,
I in them and you in me, . . . so that the world may know that
you . . . have loved them even as you have loved me" (John
17:22–23).

Thinking "peace," saying "peace," and even being *for* peace
will never be enough. I must be *of* peace, refashioned down to
the very DNA of my inner self, to be the living presence of the
peace of the reign of God.

Touching the reign of God in my life . . .

- How would I describe my response to fear, greed, and unrest in the world today? In what ways do I participate in the world's fear, greed, and unrest?

- What circumstances of fear, greed, and unrest in my own life come to mind?

- What specifically would it take for me to shift from being "for peace" to being "of peace," if I have not experienced this shift already?

- What Scriptures or teachings of my Christian heritage shed light or offer a meaningful way to reflect on circumstances of unrest and peace in my life?

- What are some key words, images, phrases, feelings, or expressions of prayer that come forward for me at this time?

Index of Scripture

Hebrew Scriptures

Genesis
1:26–27 — 76
1:27 — 33

Exodus 30:7–8 — 80

Leviticus
26:3ff — 33
26:12 — 33

Deuteronomy 6:5 — 77

2 Samuel
12:9a — 74
12:13a, b — 74

Psalm
16:4a — 84
27:8–9 — 44
51:3–4 — 74
51:7–8 — 74
51:10–11 — 74
51:13 — 75
51:15 — 73, 75
84:1 — 4
88:9 — 81
116:3–4 — 53
116:7–8 — 53
116:16 — 63
130:3f — 36
141:2 — 79

Jeremiah 20:9 — 57

Ezekiel 36:22–28 — 33

Zechariah 8:8 — 33

Apocrypha

Sirach 28:7 — 33

Christian Scriptures

Matthew
5–7 — 84
18:21 — 36
18:35 — 36
22:37 — 77

Mark
1:22, 27 — 39
12:28–34 — xi
12:34 — v
14:22–24 — 40

Luke
1:43 — 34
1:46 — 77
17:21 — v

John
1:1–5 — 40
1:14a — 76
3:16 — 35

John (*cont.*)
6:67   84
6:68   84
14:6   84
17:21   5
17:22–23   91
20:24–25   35
21:18   81

Romans
5:8   4, 40
8:26   51, 83
8:27   55
8:29   4
10:8   v
14:7–8   4, 35

1 Corinthians
6:20   41
7:23   41

2 Corinthians
5:15   32
5:18   40
5:21   41, 64

Galatians 2:20   58, 68

Ephesians 2:13–16   89

Philippians
2:5–11   20
2:6   21
2:6–8   31, 63
2:9   64

Colossians 1:15   31

Hebrews 4:12   58

1 Peter 4:8   67

1 John
1:1–3   v
4:7   68
4:11–12   68